Management Teams

Also by this author

Team Roles at Work
The Coming Shape of Organization
Changing the Way We Work
Beyond the Team
Managing Without Power

Management Teams

Why They Succeed or Fail

Third edition

R. Meredith Belbin MA PhD CCIPD FRSA

ELSEVIER

AMSTERDAM • BOSTON • HEIDELBERG • LONDON • NEW YORK • OXFORD
PARIS • SAN DIEGO • SAN FRANCISCO • SINGAPORE • SYDNEY • TOKYO

Butterworth-Heinemann is an imprint of Elsevier

Butterworth-Heinemann is an imprint of Elsevier
Linacre House, Jordan Hill, Oxford OX2 8DP, UK
30 Corporate Drive, Suite 400, Burlington, MA 01803, USA

First edition 1981
Reprinted 1983, 1984, 1985, 1986, 1987, 1988, 1989, 1990, 1991, 1992, 1993 (twice),
1994, 1995, 1996, 1997, 1998, 1999, 2000, 2002 (twice)
Second edition 2004
Reprinted 2004, 2005, 2006, 2007
Third edition 2010

British Library Cataloguing in Publication Data
A catalogue record for this book is available from the British Library

Library of Congress Cataloging-in-Publication Data
A catalog record for this book is available from the Library of Congress

ISBN: 978-1-85617-807-5

For information on all Butterworth-Heinemann publications
visit our Web site at www.books.elsevier.com

Printed and bound in Great Britain

10 11 12   10 9 8 7 6 5 4 3

Contents

Foreword

Meredith Belbin's research into the nature, structure and behaviour of teams makes for fascinating reading about the contrasting but complementary roles of the individuals who compose them.

But Meredith's work is more than fascinating; it is also extremely timely. For too many years the search for successful management has been seen almost exclusively as a search for the right individual. Organisations have been preoccupied with the qualifications, experience, and achievement of individuals; they have discussed and debated the strengths and weaknesses of individuals; and yet all of us know in our hearts that the ideal individual for a given job cannot be found. He cannot be found because he cannot exist.

Any attempt to list the qualities of a good manager demonstrates why he cannot exist: far too many of them are mutually exclusive. He must be highly intelligent and he must not be too clever. He must be forceful and he must be sensitive to people's feelings. He must be a fluent communicator and a good listener. He must be decisive and he must be reflective and so on. And if you do find this jewel amongst managers, this paragon of mutually incompatible characteristics, what will you do when he steps under a bus or goes to live abroad for the sake of his wife's health, or leaves to take up a better job from your principle competitor?

But if no individual can combine all these qualities, a team of individuals certainly can – and often does; moreover, the whole team is unlikely to step under a bus simultaneously. This is why it is not the individual but the team that is the instrument of sustained and enduring success in management. A team can renew and regenerate itself by new recruitment as individual team members leave or retire, and it can find within itself all those conflicting characteristics that cannot be united in any single individual. It can build up a store of shared and collectively owned experience, information and judgement, and this store can be passed on as seniors depart and juniors arrive. And it can be in ten places at once.

Many of us must have perceived something of the truth about teams from our own experience. We know how often someone who has been highly successful within a team becomes a great disappointment when moved out of it. We have seen effective teams destroyed by the promotion of individuals, while nobody ever considered the alternative possibility of promoting the whole team, or enlarging its scope and responsibility. And we have also seen teams produce a quality and quantity of work far higher than the sum of what the separate individuals could have produced on their own.

This is a truth known to all of us who have ever worked in successful teams. The corollary is that, while not ignoring or neglecting the individual, we should devote far

What transpired 40 years later is the language of Team Roles regularly used world-wide in large organisations. It gave a method of measuring and advising individuals, teams, and organisations about their behavioural propensities. It also offered possible solutions.

Exactly how this was achieved is a longer story. We go back in time to the end of the 1960s and the beginnings of almost a decade of research at Henley Management College.

A study of teams: how it all began

One day an unknown visitor came to our offices in Cambridge to discuss computer applications in management. There must have been many better places to pursue the matter, for we knew little about the subject. It was not even one that attracted us, although at the time it was very much the fashion.

Gradually it transpired that an application had been made for research funds to study the use of the computer in management, that the unofficial answer was a shake of the head but with a nod that pointed in our direction. If the project could be tied up in some way with the current research programme of the Industrial Training Research, the grant was more likely to be forthcoming. Why that should have been suggested is not clear; but that at any rate was how I met my future colleague, Ben Aston. Through his initiative and persuasion, a research link was established between the Industrial Training Research Unit at Cambridge and the Henley Management College.

Henley, as it is referred to more succinctly, has the distinction of being the oldest Management College in Europe, and is situated at the point where the Chiltern Hills tumble down towards the Thames. The College is the former home of Lord Hambleden and is a mile or so from the village that bears his name – a village that looks like a stage set for a period play but which is perhaps better known to Henley members for the relaxing atmosphere of its village pub.

To drive up to this stately home over the cattle grid, by the gatehouse, past the meadows dotted with low-branching trees, towards the fine close-cropped lawns that amble down to the banks of the Thames, where swans, ducks, and wild geese noisily stake out their territories in the river against the backdrop of deserted pastures beyond; all that is to heighten man's ingenuity for finding a reason for staying a little longer than was originally intended.

But it transpired that there were more basic reasons for prolonging what might otherwise have been a fleeting visit. Henley's approach to the education of managers was founded on syndicate work. A syndicate comprised of 10 or 11 members, carefully selected to give a balance in terms of background and experience. They were bankers, engineers, accountants, scientists, civil servants, and men with general production or other, setting up an experience in learning which was useful for the members. The members responded positively to the early stages of experiment at a time when we felt we knew very little. As knowledge grew, we were able to put over an account of previous work together with a tentative set of general hypotheses about the characteristics of good and poor teams. Then more constraints became necessary if we were to advance our knowledge further.

Some received the stricter design features of our experiments with good humour, interest, and fascination. A few others, it must be said, expressed from time to time the feeling that they were being manipulated, or even acted upon by sinister forces not entirely within their control. Some were displeased on the contrasting grounds that man was unpredictable, and that such experiments attempted to falsely categorise. But nearly every course contained some surprise and that offered consolation for this group!

When, in stage 4, we allowed teams to have greater participation in the selection of members, the response was at first very positive. Inviting members to form their own superteam fired their imagination. The success of the members' team, which was usually composed to take account of what we had already taught them about team composition, was a form of self-vindication. *They* too could produce impressive results by creating teams of good design. But the elitist nature of this exercise produced some internal tensions in the course from which we, the experimenters, as bystanders, escaped. These tensions prompted a modification.

A new procedure was set up to allow *all* the companies in the management game to be picked by members nominated by each syndicate. This allowed selectors to fashion their own theories on team composition. The team selectors would meet on one fateful occasion to put into operation a team selection strategy in competition with the others. To enable them to do this, the selectors had before them a set of scores based on assessments. In the later stages of the experiments, we were even able to offer them information on the Team Role characteristics of every member on the course. We have as yet, however, to introduce Team Roles (this will come in later chapters). So for now we will focus on the psychometric assessments that we provided.

The published summary assessments were presented by anonymous code numbers rather than by name. At selection time, the selectors had no idea of the identity of the coded persons. They would examine the total list and, in turn, they would pick the sort of people they thought would fit in with the team they were trying to create. The outcome could be a great shock for some selectors where their concept of team design depended on personal likes or dislikes. A favourite golfing companion would be omitted, whereas a member with whom a selector had clashed might be included. The advantage lay with those selectors who had thought about team design and balance in a more conceptual way.

The innovations and departures from our carefully planned experiments offered more involvement and participation, and provided a good deal of enjoyment for members. That gain was, however, made at a certain cost. Personal experience was vivid but on some courses at least, less of general transferable value was learned. They would not be able to learn, for example, the great disadvantages of particular combinations, and the advantages of others. Some of the members began to feel this themselves. We were pressed to return to our former and more contentious role of picking the teams according to our own design plans. 'Leave it to the experts and see what they come up with,' or words to that effect, began to be expressed in a regular and recurring way.

Selecting teams via more complex methods

Our final stage let us produce teams with carefully selected and very interesting design characteristics. Once more the outcomes were accounted for in terms of the differing compositions of the teams and whether or not they played to their strengths. We now knew far more about success and failure in teams. However, as we put forward our notions with greater confidence, levity fell and discomfiture increased – not on all sides but, as might be expected, in the teams that turned in poor performances. Acceptable excuses are readily found for team failures when work is at a tentative phase. Once knowledge became firmer, the failure of a company could produce a sense of unease or even resentment. Our own role in the proceedings and outcome was exaggerated. Some felt that our ability to forecast – even though the nature of the forecast at that stage was unknown to them – could in some way restrict their power to control their own destinies.

After 9 years of almost continuous work, we felt we had explored every twist and turn that we could think of in designing management teams, and we were beginning to rediscover and re-experience phenomena that we had first encountered a good deal earlier. In our final exercise at Henley, we made a very close prediction of the order of success and failure in the eight companies taking part. The time had come to take our leave.

Henley has a sister college in Australia, the Administrative Staff College at Melbourne, which was keen to avail itself of knowledge on the theory of the composition of effective management teams. This link resulted in three Australian tours during which the full range of team designs were tried out. Management teams 'down under' behaved like their counterparts on the other side of the world. Team design stood out as a more important determinant of behaviour than hemisphere or cultural differences.

What follows in this book is an attempt to bring out the salient points about what has been learned. Experiments and industrial applications taken together at least allow some answers to the question 'Why do some management teams succeed and others fail?'

Flaws in Apollo teams

The Apollo team members had spent a large part of their time engaged in abortive debate, trying to persuade the other members of the team to adopt their own particular, well-stated point of view. No one seemed to convert another or be converted. However, each seemed to have a flair for spotting the weak points of the other's argument. There was, not surprisingly, no coherence in the decisions that the team reached – or was forced to reach – and several pressing and necessary jobs were totally neglected. The eventual failure of the company, in finishing last in the exercise, was marked by mutual recriminations. Altogether, the Apollo company of supposed supertalent proved an astonishing disappointment.

Promising experiments always need to be repeated. For several years we continued to construct an Apollo company to participate in the EME. Of 25 companies that we constructed according to our Apollo design, only three became the winning team. The favourite finishing position out of eight was sixth (six times), followed by fourth (four times). It amazed many Henley members that companies comprising clever people (and who were recognized as such) should collectively perform so poorly.

The occasional good result, the reason for which we will examine later, redeemed the scene. However, on average, Apollo companies did perform worse than other companies in spite of their obvious advantages.

The Apollo syndrome also became an established phenomenon in the Teamopoly game that became a feature of the seminars we ran on management teams. If there was a chance of constructing a typical Apollo company, we never failed to seize it. We were seldom disappointed with the lessons that Apollo companies taught both their own members and the ever-interested onlookers from other companies.

Apollo companies usually ran true to type – difficult to manage, prone to destructive debate, and difficulties with decision-making. Members of these companies acted along lines that they favoured personally, without taking account of what fellow company members were doing. This at least circumvented the blockages caused by collective indecision, but unco-ordinated action is only slightly better than taking no action at all. What one member did was undermined, usually unintentionally, by the actions of another. The lack of coherent teamwork nullified the gains of individual effort or brilliance. Apollo companies were frequently in cash flow problems in Teamopoly due to the competing strategic demands for whatever cash the company had.

Occasionally, the behaviour of Apollo companies did not follow the typical pattern. Yet they still failed to fulfil their potential. Perhaps they had heard of and were overconscious of the dangers. In these instances, Apollo members seemed deliberately to avoid their susceptibility to intellectual rivalry and one-upmanship.

They showed undue respect for each other's proposals. Confrontation was avoided by the reluctance to admit that some proposals were mutually incompatible. This overcompensation in behaviour had a similar effect to engaging in confrontation and then ignoring the opposition, albeit a cosier one. In both instances, ideas were left hanging in the air and no one understood how the various contributions had been assimilated and to what end.

The NASA Apollo team

Some time after our experiments, the Apollo team was brought to life in a particularly ironic manner. Dr. David Marriott from Australia and I had received a contract from NASA to provide an educational input into the performance of their teams. The key problem in the organisation was one of highly talented individuals failing to work as effectively as a team as the mission desired.

What happened next was a classic illustration of the Apollo effect. Amongst the individuals themselves, they could not even come to an agreement to go ahead with the seminar. So our work, designed to help them, was stopped before it could start. Having already been contracted to do the work, I was awarded a cancellation fee before even starting on the journey.

Successful Apollo teams

Some Apollo companies did achieve reasonably good results and these exceptions to the rule are not without interest since they give us leads on how think-tank teams might be formed – should that objective be considered worth pursuing.

One useful lead on the possible construction of Apollo companies came from the experience of allowing members to form a team of their own design. This occurred at a stage in the work when members had been given some practical guides on the principles of team composition. The guide was given based on our research. Representatives from the syndicates would then meet to nominate members for one Superteam. After that we formed the remaining members into other competing companies.

The representatives made their nominations on the basis of what they personally knew about the members and not, of course, on the basis of the test results, which were not available to them. Using a strict definition of an Apollo company, only one of the six Superteams was an Apollo and this company finished third. However, there were three other Superteams that just fell short of our Apollo criterion, of which two finished first and one third. The other two non-Apollo teams were both winners.

The members' Superteams not only achieved good results, but also succeeded in avoiding the Apollo pitfalls. While the electing members took account of team-building principles, they also engaged in a number of initiatives of their own making. Superteam members were chosen for their particular skills (in numeracy, in co-ordinating ability, or in control) and thereby some measure of interdependence was built up. In addition, some sophisticated thought was put into ways of correcting the imbalance in the Superteam, which those selecting it had begun to suspect might be its problem.

In one instance, a selector proposed somebody for the Superteam who was seen as the joker in the pack, who would take the tension out of the situation. The person he had in mind was a former Welsh international rugby forward, now known as a real prankster. Such foresight was rewarded exactly in the way expected. In other cases, clever but very awkward members were excluded from the Superteam on the grounds that they might give more trouble than they were worth. By giving careful consid-eration to all the personal characteristics of members, selectors seemed capable of forming better-balanced and more successful teams. These were signs that this approach could extend to Apollo and near-Apollo teams too.

Another feature of successful Apollo teams was the absence of highly dominant individuals apart from the Chairman. The combination of a high score on the Critical Thinking Appraisal (CTA) and a low score on the Assertive scale of the Personality Inventory was especially favourable. The only danger here was that such members might sit back and play a passive role unless there was someone present to pull the whole thing together.

Perhaps the main key to the successful Apollo team was the character of the Chairman. But the good Apollo Chairman did not behave in the same way as the Chairman of other successful teams. In Chapter 5 this is discussed in some detail. Suffice it here to say that clever people seem to need leadership of a different style and type from people who are not so gifted.

Although Apollo teams could turn out very well, it was more usual for them to yield disappointing results. Outcomes were always difficult to forecast since differences between success and failure depended on factors that were often no more than marginal. Apollo companies usually had all the talent, at least in a technical sense, that was needed if only they knew how to use it.

Explanations of results

Let us consider in more detail why the general run of Apollo companies performed so indifferently.

The first explanation is that all members of an Apollo company are inclined to have the same aspirations, i.e. to apply their critical minds to the most difficult and intellectually enticing parts of the exercise. This is borne out by the high scores which the observers recorded in these companies for those items of behaviour covered in 'proposing' and 'opposing' – putting forward ideas and pointing out the flaws in others' proposals. The emphasis was on analysis and counter-analysis. Certainly these are very important aspects of a team's activities, when faced with a set of interlocking problems; but there are other aspects that are equally important and which may be neglected. Using resources, collecting and exchanging information, recording what is known, co-ordinating plans, and action all have a vital part to play in helping to make a team effective.

Some may argue that this explanation is no explanation. Why should Apollo members restrict their behaviour in this way? Why should they limit their role more than members of other companies?

A possible answer lies in the very pressures that our educational system and culture exert on clever people. Those who at school are 'top of the class', or who have it within their reach, are continually being judged in terms of their scholastic pre-eminence. To come second is to fail. Beating the next person is the name of the game. Difficult problems excite the greatest rivalry and so destroy the bonds of mutual co-operation and complementary functioning upon which the success of a team ultimately depends. In other words, overconcentration on coming top of the class provides an unconscious training in anti-teamwork.

There is another by-product of intellectual sharpness that may also cause difficulties for teams and provide, therefore, a second explanation of the factors underlying Apollo misfortunes. Membership of Apollo companies was contingent on securing a high score on the CTA. The word 'critical', as applied to the mind, has two meanings in the English language. One meaning denotes mental acumen or analytical powers. The second meaning implies a negative evaluation: a critical mind aims to find fault in another's argument or to look for and perceive shortcomings and blemishes.

High critical thinkers, we were to learn, tended to have critical minds in both senses of the word. The negative side of their perceptions was indicated by a characteristic of their scores on the test that we developed at Cambridge called the PPQ (see Glossary). The PPQ was a way of establishing what particular subjects concerned the respondent, by asking them to rate two famous people and to explain why they believed one to be better than the other. Each way of judging was termed a 'construct', and the different constructs of an individual proved to be highly informative about what made him or her tick.

The PPQ marking procedure allowed for a ratio of positive and negative constructs to be scored for each respondent. In the event, high critical thinkers (as judged on the CTA) were found to have a high negative construct ratio (as judged on the PPQ). In other words, clever people were finding more negative things to say about the world at large, making them appear to have a negative outlook.

Do negative constructs mean a negative approach? Not necessarily. Negative constructs can be part of discrimination. To arrive at a worthwhile decision, it may be a useful tactic to consider and dispose of all unwanted alternatives. A high proportion of negative constructs may, however, have a damaging effect on social intercourse and interfere with good team integration.

The Apollo syndrome in practice

Once we had fully explored Apollo phenomena in the Henley management game and in Teamopoly, we began to look around for counterparts in the broader world. The most likely places in which to encounter Apollo groups are areas where clever people congregate. High-technology groups that need to recruit well-qualified and able individuals, the boards of companies that place great faith in rapid promotion on the basis of performance, and specially convened committees and working groups whose members are selected for their creative ability and expertise are just the places where one might expect difficulty.

Difficulties much like those reported in our experiments were reported to us as being very prevalent in hospital management. The key figures in hospitals are consultants and no major decisions can be made without their involvement. Meetings of hospital consultants have a certain notoriety for their failure to move smoothly to rational decisions in spite of the undoubted talents of their members. One well-informed source considers that the resulting problem underlies the tendency of the National Health Service to over-react by recruiting too many administrators!

It is difficult to assess whether a firm is likely to be prone to the Apollo syndrome without having hard data on the mental abilities of senior managers and directors. This is not easily obtained. Those in high office are often enthusiastic about administering tests, including intelligence tests, to those they are considering recruiting, but they are less than enthusiastic about taking the same tests themselves. Inevitably, therefore, we are left to infer rather more than we would like about the individual abilities of members of teams observed in the industrial and commercial world.

There are two areas of industry where high mental ability is considered ahead of any of the other personal characteristics that recommend candidates for responsible appointments: one of these lies in computer applications and the other in the field of research and development.

As it happened, my colleague Roger Mottram and I both found ourselves engaged in examining team-building problems in each of these areas soon after we had discovered the Apollo syndrome, he looking at the computer field while I concentrated on research and development. The small teams that Mottram studied operated within a large firm engaged in installing computer hardware and systems for customers. He tested the members of these teams and found the majority of them to be high critical thinkers. Some of the cleverest teams turned out to be the least successful – especially where the project manager was himself the cleverest and most creative member. It was at the level of communication that these project teams were often most vulnerable: communications were poor both within the team and with clients. Rearrangement of the teams so that a more managerial but less creative member acted as project leader was associated with a considerable gain in team effectiveness without any loss of the technical and creative capability of the team as a whole.

Experience with firms that invest heavily in research and development has added to our understanding of Apollo phenomenon in terms of what can go wrong. Teams containing the cleverest members show remarkable resistance to any form of imposed organisation. Exactly why this should be so is not clear. We did not notice any such tendency during our experimental work, but then there were no organisational pressures imposed from outside. The nearest parallel was the tendency to disorganisation evident within the team. Two instances illustrate the liking of Apollo-type teams for socially satisfying but anarchic autonomy.

CASE STUDY – HIGH INTELLECT COUPLED WITH DISORGANISATION

A firm specializing in contract research and development and known to be the largest of its kind in the UK made every effort (with the use of tests) to recruit very clever research scientists. The policy was well rewarded and the firm prospered. At first, organisation was no problem. Everyone gave a hand in whatever way was most fitting to deal with the small but steady stream of contracts that came in. Income and expenditure were balanced in the most informal way. As these scientists were mainly interested in their work, questions of relating extrinsic rewards to contribution scarcely claimed their attention. It was not a problem when everyone lent a hand to make a success of a project.

But as more research contracts were placed, the scientists needed to divide their responsibilities in a more equitable fashion so that each took the work most appropriate to particular skills and abilities. Some projects went better than others and in the case of fixed price contracts, it became clear that the company was making a good deal of profit on some contracts, while losing money on projects giving difficulty.

The stage had now been reached when some administrative function was needed at managerial level if the company was to meet its commitments, make a profit, and prosper generally. All recognized this and also that such work was not to their liking, and that an entirely different species of human being was required to cope with the work envisaged.

In due course, the company found an appropriate manager with the requisite experience and personal qualities. The new manager soon got down to work drawing up forms upon which essential information could be gathered for the purpose of financial control. To enable the company to quote a price for a contract more accurately than it had done in the past, a record was needed of the number of hours that each scientist devoted to each project. The minutes were immaterial. Even a global estimate of the hours spent on projects would furnish the controllers with all the information required to improve the company's profitability.

The system never worked. It failed at the start. Creative scientists did not see themselves wasting their valuable time filling in forms. Worse, they began to develop some antagonism to the petty-minded manager, as they saw him, who demanded the information.

Filled with frustration, the manager left. The company now regressed to its blissful bohemian existence, only to run deeper into the problems that had called for such an appointment in the first place. This time it was resolved that an appointment should be made of a manager who was a scientist rather than a professional administrator, but a scientist with a flair for organisation.

Eventually a very interesting candidate was found with a particular interest in the commercial side of operations. This man seemed to have everything that was needed and he soon found himself prominently placed near the apex of the company. Unfortunately, as his influence grew and even as the company found its trading position improving, a cleavage began to develop and then widen between this organised individual and the original boffins who had made the company what it was. The point was reached when the manager began to feel that life could be more comfortable in another company. A new opportunity beckoned and the company was left once again in its primeval state.

The second example deals with a manufacturing company with a very heavy expenditure in research and development. Long-established and more traditional companies develop a culture in which the needs for systems and organisation are appreciated and those who run them have a certain social standing. What happens then when an Apollo group forms in such a company?

Why should Apollo members get into such a tizzy about authority, management, leadership, and organisation? It is difficult to think of any fundamental personality reasons why this should be so. Examination of the test scores of high critical thinkers showed that they came in all shapes and sizes: introverted, extroverted, dominant, recessive, anxious, stable, and so on.

CASE STUDY – AN APOLLO TEAM DOMINATED BY HIERARCHY

This large company was separated into a number of semi-autonomous divisions, each of which maintained its own research and development effort, while at the same time drawing on a corporate laboratory. In one of the divisions with a particularly heavy research and development budget, there emerged a scientist with such a breadth of talent that he soon found himself figuring prominently in all those wider, more managerial questions with which a research department ultimately becomes embroiled. At the same time, there was about him a touch of the maverick. Such a man is almost safer occupying a position of responsibility than criticizing play from the sidelines.

In due course, after he had reached as high a position in the hierarchy as he could without removing the current incumbents, it was realized that some career path would have to be made for him, either within the division or in the company as a whole. He was young enough to consider an appointment outside research; but on the other hand, his seniority made it difficult to find the appropriate slot. In career terms, what he now needed was to be given free reign in a position of greater responsibility than that which he had already held.

After a short absence from the company, I returned to inquire what had happened to our friend. Yes, he had gone from the research department. An appointment had been found for him at the company's corporate laboratory. His scientific experience was too valuable to lose; yet, he needed fresh fields to conquer.

Naturally, I was interested to learn more about the position he had taken up. The answer came as something of a surprise. 'He will be a senior man at the corporate laboratory working with the research manager.' The deputy research manager? 'No, not exactly. By that I don't mean he won't be the deputy research manager. He will be but he mustn't be called it. You see the scientists there recognize the authority of the research manager but they will not recognize the authority of anyone under him. It makes it difficult. Someone has to do the job but without having the benefit of the title.'

Interaction in Apollo teams

One possibility arises from the difficulties caused by the tendency of clever people to overvalue cleverness. High scorers on the CTA showed a marked inclination to be strongly influenced by 'brain' constructs on the PPQ, especially negative brain constructs. In other words, those with high mental ability showed both that they admired intelligence and that they did not suffer fools gladly.

This respect and need for other clever people like themselves can create diffi-culty. If they find the colleagues they are seeking, they are likely to find themselves making similar and therefore competing contributions. This easily leads to a loss in role identity and so to role confusion. The question of leadership aggravates the problem. To the high critical thinker, with his outlook governed by 'brain' constructs, leadership is often taken to mean the ability to analyse the problem and point to the solution. In the eyes of rank-and-file but clever members of a team, there is little distinction between what they see as their role and what they see as the leader's role.

The manager's concept of his or her own responsibility for making decisions directly conflicts, or is capable of doing so, with the cleverest member's natural aptitude for evaluating problems. Managers are probably more concerned with synthesis than analysis. They are often supplied with a great deal of pre-analysed material; their function is to make a balanced decision having regard to all factors in a situation, including human factors. A manager needs a fair measure of mental ability but that may not be the most important requirement for the job.

If Apollo members find themselves competing for some aspects of the leadership role without being able to discharge that role in its broader sense, they are likely to disrupt, rather than contribute to, the effective functioning of the group. The points at issue they raise will not be readily resolved. Debating skills do not bind people together. If anything, they cause and open up rifts and divisions.

The Apollo syndrome refers to a phenomenon found in groups whose members are chosen primarily for their critical thinking faculties, whereby destructive tendencies come to the fore and result in an underachievement by the team as a whole. People with high analytical abilities are not necessarily creative. High mental ability does, however, imply some ability to produce ideas.

Good ideas take time to develop. They demand favourable conditions. There may be men with ideas in an Apollo company but the Apollo company is not the place where a person gifted with creative ability is likely to flourish. An Apollo team is not, therefore, in any effective sense a creative team.

Summary

- Contrary to expectations, Apollo teams were generally the worst performers.
- High levels of competition and negativity and the tendency to tear down others' ideas damaged the team's efforts.
- Significant activities were ignored by the Apollo teams, who preferred debate.
- Those Apollo teams that succeeded were those that were conscious of their team composition.

Stable Extroverts are known to fulfil themselves and excel in jobs that place a premium on liaison work and where cooperation is sought from others. They flourish as sales representatives and do well in personnel management.

Anxious Extroverts are commonly found where people need to work at a high pace and exert pressure on others. Anxious extroversion seems to confer an occupational advantage among sales managers, works managers, and editors.

Stable Introverts seem to do well in work where good relationships with a small number of people need to be maintained over a period. They flourish as administrators, solicitors, local and central government officials, and as corporate planners in industry.

Anxious Introverts distinguish themselves in jobs that call for self-direction and self-sustaining persistence. They predominate among research scientists and among specialists committed to long-term assignments. Some of the most creative people belong to this group.

Individuals within any one occupational grouping naturally vary in personality. Nevertheless, the deliberate creation of homogenous management teams in personality terms meant, in practice, creating teams drawn from one occupational field. Stable Extrovert (SE) teams contained, as expected, an undue proportion of people in Sales, Marketing, and Personnel: they were often short of members with skills in numeracy and we could seldom find members in Engineering or Research and Development functions who could be put into the team. For Anxious Introvert (AI) teams, we found quite a few eligible accountants to add to the expected quota of researchers. The difficulty now was that the AI teams tended to have superfluous personnel who were notable for their numeracy skills.

Teams of Anxious Extroverts (AEs) and Stable Introverts (SIs) also had their own distinctive characteristics. AE teams were not difficult to form, for they were supplied with a good cross-section of managers covering a wide range of functions; but well to the fore were General Managers, followed by Managers of Management Services, and a sprinkling of bankers. For some reason, however, there was an insufficiency of members suitable for SI teams.

The lack of SIs on courses being run for senior managers may suggest that not many SIs progress into the higher echelons of management. Or it could be that they keep away from management courses. These two possibilities are not mutually exclusive. It is a fair guess that pure SIs, though very employable and efficient in a functional sense, are prone to passivity and overcontentment. This could reduce their sense of need to develop themselves through further education in management and possibly lessen the likelihood of their reaching top positions.

The exceptions we came across were individuals with very high scores in mental ability. These managers did not have the typical managerial temperament or the need for achievement but they did seem actuated by a sense of intellectual quest and enquiry. As managers, they made their mark as strategic thinkers.

Although our teams of SEs, AEs, SIs, and AIs were not perfectly balanced in occupational background or mental ability, they had a distinctive quality of their own which seemed to emerge irrespective of the different contexts and demands of the EME and Teamopoly. They also, significantly, showed characters as teams that went beyond the different sources of information by means of which we learnt about their characters as individuals.

In the case of the EME we had independent observer notes and reports, sometimes copious, to guide us, while for Teamopoly we had to rely on our own observations supplemented by the reports from the members of the companies themselves at the public inquest on the final day. In this latter case, members engaged in this self-revelation were remarkably perceptive about themselves and their colleagues, often hilariously so. From these observations, a picture began to emerge of the typical styles of work that our four sets of companies were prone to adopt.

Pure teams – their successes and failures

Putting together our teams constructed entirely of one of our four combinations, brought out extremes of behaviour and effect. In general, purely extroverted teams tended to have a higher rate of success than purely introverted ones, but there were differences in results and each group had both strengths and inherent problems.

Comparing success in two different games

The results from our experiments with pure teams gave an overall idea of how our pure teams performed in conditions that closely simulated real-world business. However, there were differences in performance between the two games, a first decisive indication that there is no one perfect team. Instead, different forms of teams tended to come across different obstacles or to excel in different circumstances.

The SE companies did particularly well in the EME (see Chapter 8). The differences between the other three companies were small. The AEs were marginally better than the SIs, while the AIs were rather prone to be the lowest scorers. Where they did achieve an above average result, this was usually due to the performance of one star member. In Teamopoly, AEs were more successful than the SEs, while both teams tended to have the upper hand over the SIs and the AIs.

While we could attribute some of the difference in scores between EME and Teamopoly to the varying requirements of the two games, some additional factors

Yet another resource that SE companies used to advantage was the record sheets produced by the observers. The observers were under instruction neither to volunteer the information they were collecting nor to keep it back if people wanted to see it. SE companies often took an interest in what was going on, with the result that company style was sometimes modified so as to make it more effective.

Perhaps the most striking use of resources, however, was illustrated by the response of an SE company to the possibility of using an operational research consultant.

CASE STUDY – STABLE EXTROVERTS USE OF RESOURCES

Tom Child, seconded to the College on a research project, had a specialized knowledge of mathematical models as they affect business operations. It seemed quite appropriate that he should be available as a resource during the EME. At the same time it was agreed with the organisers that he would not be allowed to solve personally any problems that a company in the exercise brought to the fore. Accordingly, the consultant did his rounds at the start of one exercise, explaining what help he might offer. The reception he received was something less than warm. The equivocal nature of his help as a consultant was seen by some companies as being irritating. Tom was referred to as high-handed and aggravating; and other less than complimentary words were registered by the observers as being applied to him by aggrieved interviewers.

The SE team's reaction to Tom Child was of a different order. He was received by the company as a whole and after various questions had been posed and answers given, it was agreed that one of their number should keep in contact with him. Tom responded to what seemed to him a cordial reception in a positive fashion. While the help given to this company remained indirect, the hints, clues, and leads offered turned out to be ample reward for the patience expended. The SE company cheerfully modified its policy – without quite fully understanding what it was doing – and was delighted to find its fortunes bound upwards to give it the lead in financial performance. It was a lead they failed to consolidate, but by the final session they were still strongly placed.

Lessons of results

The four pure companies we have been considering all had merits, which gave them advantages in particular situations. But they were also susceptible to particular weaknesses. Our SE companies, for example, were prone to make small errors, which in their easy-going way they failed to note or rectify. Because the members of these companies had much in common, the natural balancing qualities found in groups with diverse members were absent. Nevertheless, groups with similar types of members are usually able to find a style of operation that suits all the members.

It may be argued that in the industrial and commercial world pure companies never exist. Even if a company wished to recruit in its own image, it would have difficulty in doing so since chance factors bring forward all manner of people eligible for the vacancies that arise. Against this is a view that some firms cultivate a culture that is close to one of the four basic personality types and that such a culture exercises an overriding effect on personal behaviour, at least in so far as it is expressed within the firm. For example, parallels have been drawn between the typical AE companies as observed in our experiments and certain newspaper groups in the publishing world. In the same way, SI cultures are found in local government, and AI cultures in research.

As it happens, individuals belonging to these organisations commonly fit into the personality pattern that might be naturally expected from them. Yet this is not always the case. Inevitably, a certain amount of misfit does occur. In these cases, behaviour within the organisation is more likely to accord with the 'personality' of the culture than with the natural personality of the individual. In this respect, so-called national characteristics should not be dismissed as stereotypes, for they reflect the culture of which the stereotype is itself a product.

This point is well brought out by multinational companies. The value of such companies is that they can transport a culture overseas, assimilating foreign nationals in the process and so maintaining the impetus and dynamism of the parent. Naturally, this very strength is a source of the resentment which multinationals attract. What is forgotten is that the culture lies at the very heart of what a company is able to achieve.

CASE STUDY – A SUCCESSFUL CORPORATE COMPANY RUN ALONG STABLE EXTROVERT LINES

A good example of a thriving SE company in a foreign land is Mars Ltd. and its subsidiary, Petfoods Ltd. Mars is a privately owned American company with a larger turnover in the UK than in the US. The employees of Mars are highly paid and there are no trade unions. When Mars was set up on the Slough Trading Estate, its style created something of a cultural shock. It was as though it had been deliberately designed to counter the insularity of managers and the loss of communication which excessive social stratification engenders in traditionally run English firms. Offices were organised on an open plan; managers and workers used the same canteen. An employee could walk into the personnel manager's office at any time to air a grievance. Coats were taken off when discussions took place. Christian names were prevalent. Open management, free communications, and buddy relationships were fostered. The culture has also influenced the selection process. Graduates are expected to perform well in group discussion and generally to show strong ability in the capacity to communicate. Those who are recruited to Mars may not all be SEs, but if they behave like SEs they are likely to contribute to the continued progress of the firm along lines that are already proven.

The pure types of company, which formed the design basis of our experimental management teams, were chosen because these parameters of behaviour were measurable, with tests, and were already known to have an important bearing on performance. There was no reason for presuming, however, that choosing members of a team could only be done using the four categories. There were perhaps other team types that could prove more effective and interesting. This was all the more worth exploring as there were many members who could not be fitted into one of the pure companies, because they themselves did not conform to any one type.

Personality and the effective Implementer

We looked next to see if we could identify a team member common to successful teams. The approach was to examine the 16PF test scores (see Glossary) of members of teams that had gained good results in the EME, and then to compare them with the scores of those belonging to companies that had suffered poor financial results.

Isolating those factors that were the best differentiators, we grouped them into a cluster to give us the type we were looking for. We needed a name for this type; we initially called him a Company Worker, but later came to rename this individual the **Implementer** (IMP). The reasons for this are concerned with those who tended to emerge as this role. The term Company Worker does not sound very glamorous, and yet there were many high-profile managers who displayed these characteristics to great success. Although the name also shows the degree of loyalty to the company, what was missed was the taking of ideas and concepts and putting them into implementation.

Six factors were involved. IMPs were disciplined individuals with an affinity towards getting work done swiftly in an organised fashion. Conscientious and aware of external obligations, they also had a well-developed sense of self-image, giving them a degree of internal control. They were tough-minded, practical, trusting, tolerant towards others, and, finally, conservative in the sense of being respectful of established conditions and ways of looking at things.

IMPs were not simply team members who did or arranged things (most work involves both). In behavioural terms, they were people who essentially worked *for the company*, rather than in pursuit of self-interest, and did so in a practical and realistic way. They could identify with the organisation and would accept and look for goals in work that fell in line with its ideals and aspirations. There was never any question that jobs would not be done because they did not feel like it or it did not interest them.

This capacity for disciplined application was a function of the IMPs' attitude and character against which natural aptitude or intelligence seemed almost of secondary importance. Being disciplined, they would tend to have an orderly approach to the work before them. Any flair that they might possess nearly always lay in organisational ability.

In large, well-structured organisations such people become very promotable. It is an irony that, while the image of the IMP tended to have only a limited appeal to managers, the ranks of Managing Directors contained as many people with IMP affinities as with any other role. It has been claimed that the IMP characteristics is a common commodity and in consequence, surprise is expressed that IMP qualities can be associated with the highest ranks of office.

Here we would argue that ideal IMP qualities are much rarer than people realise. One definition of the Managing Director is that he or she is the manager who tackles the jobs that nobody else will do. There is a strong grain of truth in this. Many people in practice only do the sort of jobs that appeal to them and neglect those that they find distasteful. There is no great joy, for example, in disciplining a negligent employee or removing from a job someone whose work has not reached the necessary standard. IMPs succeed over a period of time because they systematically set about doing the sort of jobs that need to be done in management even though they may be far from intrinsically interesting or pleasant. This is a great test of character strength, quite at variance with what is implied by the notion of the 'organisation man'.

If this evident weakling exists in positions of responsibility, he has little in common with the IMP who has emerged from our intensive studies. Both individuals face the constraints of the system of which they are a necessary part. The difference seems to be that in the one case the individual succumbs to the pressures that the system places upon him, while in the other the individual not only meets its needs but in the process grows in stature.

Once the IMP cluster had been isolated, the scene was set for an experiment in validation. During a period of 2 years, companies competing in the EME were composed according to their IMP characteristics. There were pure companies where all members scored highly as IMPs and there were pure companies were all were low scorers on the IMP scale. Mental ability was also controlled. There were therefore IMP companies high in mental ability and IMP companies low in mental ability.

Limitations of pure Implementer teams

We expected some interesting results from these experiments, and since we had divined that companies with IMPs in their number succeeded, it was natural to assume that a team constructed of these individuals would fare well. But the results were largely negative. If IMP members were associated with good team results, then pure companies, full of IMPs, failed to produce better results than average, even in association with high mental ability. In later years, in order to double-check our findings in the EME, we tried pure IMP companies in Teamopoly and the picture was very similar.

Although our results were negative, the experiments were not deemed a failure. Our good fortune in having a few excellent observers over this period gave us a lead in the shortcomings of the pure IMP company. The IMP manager, as we have seen, was a well-organised, disciplined but tolerant, practical, and rather orthodox person. This was someone who accepted the constraints of the game and produced an unquestioning dedication to what was required. The IMP was therefore an asset to a company that was taking the exercise seriously and trying to win.

Collectively, however, IMPs did not produce good teams. Observer scores and comments presented a picture of organisation and effort but of a lack of real ideas. IMP teams were also found to be prone to inflexibility once they had established their frame of reference. They were strongly committed to anything they set in motion and were disturbed by having to change plans. They worked well but failed to get good results.

The experience with IMP companies brought to the fore the limitations of *pure* teams. Pure teams develop a style and quality of their own. If the situation matches that style, the pure company can excel. In practice there can be no guarantee that any particular situation or demand will continue in a given form. The longer a management team is exposed to the problems of the real world, the greater the need to be prepared for a full range of problems and situations, and to have the resources in a team ready to meet them.

What does emerge from the experiments described in this chapter is that teams of similar people have characteristic strengths and weaknesses. The question to carry forward – and this became the key to the entirety of the research – was 'How can the strengths be retained and the weaknesses eliminated?'

Summary

- Pure teams of one personality type were created.
- Different teams succeeded in different circumstances.
- Each pure team had strengths and weaknesses that could cause success or failure.
- One team member, the **Implementer** (IMP), was common to all successful teams but failed when put into a team of pure IMPs.

Creativity
in the team

Once the limitations to the Implementer (IMP) role were observed, our immediate concern was to ensure that the team was able to compensate for the short-comings of a successful IMP. The IMP would usually lack creativity, flexibility, and lateral thinking.

So in order to create an effective, successful team, it must not only have the organized, efficient IMP, but also be a team capable of creative thought.

Most large organisations are interested in the formation of creative teams. The favoured approach is to take an already existing team and to make it more creative than it would otherwise tend to be. 'Brainstorming' pioneered this field and later 'synectics' and 'lateral thinking' added to the repertoire of means available for encouraging a flow of ideas directed towards the solving of problems. There is no doubt that the tools now exist for enabling groups to generate ideas – and ideas in quantity. Where groups look prone to the overcritical tendencies of the Apollo syndrome, these methods have much to recommend them.

However, to what extent can a prolific flow of ideas be taken as the hallmark of the creative group? For a long time it seemed a reasonable bet that one was a fair indicator of the other. Not only does a creative group need an adequate range of ideas, but the more the members of a group contribute to their production, the greater the sense of personal involvement and identification with the object of the proceedings.

The first glimmerings of doubt about the merits of this approach began to dawn on us after close examination of the observer records during EME. It was true that some teams were held back by their inability to generate an adequate number of ideas. But these were exceptions. There was not, in contrast, the slightest tendency for greater success during the EME where there was a higher number of ideas being put forward. In fact, some of its most successful teams had a below average count on this score: they seemed well able to elicit a few good suggestions and to act on them appropriately.

This prompted us to look around industry to assess how effective were those groups that were being consciously moulded to make them 'creative'. What we thought we saw was the recurring phenomenon of a lack of ability to utilize the ideas produced. Working from the other direction, we looked at cases where important 'breakthroughs' had actually been made. What struck us in these instances was the basic simplicity of the social process. It was not the case that all the members of the team contributed to the ideas. More usually, a single individual would provide a key idea which was judged to be correct and then put into action.

Two things were beginning to become apparent here. The first: that it is not the number, but the value of the ideas suggested that produces success. In teams where a multitude of ideas are produced by those who are encouraged to 'think creatively', genuinely good ideas are often lost in a sea of conflicting points. The second: that there is a process by which good ideas are taken up. They are presented, judged to be sound, and then put into process. To put it in a single sentence: *With the right combination of people, the act of creation was effortless.*

Making use of creative ability in a team

With the benefit of this insight, we began to develop some different hypotheses about the conditions that bring about creativity in the team. We could now see obvious drawbacks in encouraging everyone in a group to become creative. Principally, there was the problem of disposing of unwanted ideas, which is part of the process of eventual arrival at those one or two ideas that are worth adopting. In practice, the most politically acceptable way of narrowing down the choices was to combine the ideas of the most dominant members. The search for compromise would soon become a matter of appeasement, with realistic objections to either proposal, or to combining proposals that were incompatible, taking second place. As a way out of this danger, some people advocate setting up two teams – one to generate ideas and the other to evaluate them. This suggestion has merits but for everyday purposes seems somewhat complicated.

The alternative strategy for encouraging all the members of a group to engage in the identical task of producing ideas (a somewhat wasteful use of manpower) is to induce a team to understand and to make better use of the individual talents of its members. Some individuals are gifted with a truly innovative turn of mind. If that talent can be recognized and harnessed, the 'noise' problem is avoided. There is no need to sift through all the ideas that can be produced. One original 'spark' can set off a new line of thought in the development of which all may find a part to play. A simple decision can then be made as to whether the resultant package is sound or not – and that can become the responsibility of a person of mature judgement.

Identifying creative potential

We now run into the problem of being able to identify this able idea maker in the first place. In the EME, the observer records showed which members had engaged in most proposing, but there was no way of knowing how good any of these proposals were. We had set in motion a system for recording which proposals were acted upon and which were ignored, whereby individuals whose ideas had proved the most productive could be traced. Unfortunately, some of our observers found themselves unable to use the method, especially when discussions lost any semblance of control or direction. It had to be abandoned as a standard method. However, we did glean enough information before this happened to find a relationship between the most prolific idea makers and the ideas that were used. The relationship suggested that we would not be too far out if we regarded the leading *proposing* rates as belonging to the most creative members.

In this way a sample was formed of people with probable creative tendencies. Their test records were then examined. We duly isolated a cluster of distinguishing characteristics only to find that the treasure trove had already been discovered by a previous explorer. Our cluster was none other than the pre-existing Cattell formula for Creative Disposition (CD). From then onwards, the CD formula was to become a valuable tool for identifying creative individuals. We adopted it as it stood, and utilised it as the means of ensuring that any team we were to compose had some creative potential within it.

> ## RAYMOND CATTELL
>
> Raymond Cattell was born in Staffordshire in 1905 and retired in 1973 at the University of Illinois, where he was research professor in psychology and director of the Laboratory of Personality and Group Behaviour Research. Cattell received all of his education in England, gaining from the University of London a BSc in Chemistry and a PhD in Psychology, later followed by a DSc in recognition of his wide scientific work. But most of his work for which he is best known was conducted in the United States, culminating in the award of the Wenner-Gren prize by the New York Academy of Science. While his name is closely associated with the dozen intelligence, personality, and clinical tests that bear his name, Cattell's written output prior to his retirement included 22 books and monographs and 235 scientific articles.
>
> Since the original *Management Teams* was published, Raymond Cattell has, however, sadly passed away. His death in 1998 was greatly mourned, but his work has been continued and built on in the decade since. His legacy is likely to last for decades to come. His inventory had a great impact on all theories of personality, and is echoed in almost all those that have come afterwards.

The Cattell Personality Inventory (16PF) has probably been more researched into, in terms of its bearing on industrial occupation categories, than any other personality measure. As far as creativity was concerned, Cattell's method was to obtain a large number of nominations of people considered creative in their particular fields, ranging over the arts and the sciences. He managed to persuade these nominees to take his personality inventory and then compared their test scores with those of the general population. They differed from the general population on 10 of the 16 scales, with the highest weightings on intelligence and tender-mindedness, and three of the scales belonging to introversion. The creative were also more dominant, socially bold, natural, imaginative, and radical.

Before we attempt to construct a picture of the typically creative individual from his test scores, it is as well to reflect on one fundamental matter. Creative ability is usually thought of as being linked in some way with measurable intelligence. Cattell's formula contains the link but it establishes something more: a creative individual has a distinctive set of personal qualities that lie embedded in his character and which do not depend on intelligence.

Although the Cattell formula fitted well with the data on individuals who created ideas in the teams we had observed, there seemed a case for cross-validating the formula on the teams we were about to construct, in this case testing the accuracy of our experience-based predictions.

Experiments with creativity

We began a series of experiments, with the aim of making predictions about the creative abilities of individuals. The predictions were based on particular sets of scores on the psychometric tests. The method was to pick out those with the highest combination of scores on mental ability – in this instance the Critical Thinking Appraisal (CTA) and Creative Disposition (CD on the Cattell formula) – and to plant each high scorer into a separate company where his or her behaviour could be recorded by an independent observer. The observer, who had no knowledge of the hypothesis underlying the experiments, was able to provide at the end of the exercise a total score on proposing ideas for the six members of each company. The scores could be arranged in rank order from the person who did the most proposing to the one who did the least.

The key individual, with the most potentially creative profile in the psychometric tests, we called the **Plant** (PL), since this person was planted for experimental purposes into the company. Technically, we had come to the conclusion that we required a score of 80 on CTA and 98 on CD. In some cases we fell just short of these qualifying figures so that those chosen were termed Subplants. Others who were almost overqualified became known as Superplants. At any rate, we ended up with one clever person (PL, Superplant or Subplant) per company. The experimental study covered 38 companies with 38 chosen PLs (or their equivalents). The identity of the PLs was not disclosed to the other team members or to the observers.

The results supported the prediction. Taking the 38 companies, each with 6 members, PLs ranked as the highest idea generators in 13 cases and second highest in 12 cases. Three of our PLs scored as third highest, whilst only one was fourth. Eight PLs were the fifth highest, the only outlying point on our chart, and only one of our PLs generated the fewest ideas. Clearly, the trend was in the expected direction and to an impressive degree. More impressive still was the way in which PLs transformed the job assigned to them in the exercise.

We had previously noted that jobs varied in terms of the opportunity that each provided for generating ideas. Members of companies who were given responsibility for Marketing produced the highest proposing rate, due to the requirements of the role. These were followed by the team's Chairman, whose position required and encouraged the proposing of ideas from time to time, and then in turn those looking after Finance, Production, and Management Services. Last was Company Secretary – this role requiring very little in the way of idea generation. From Marketing to Company Secretary there was a steep gradient so that the Marketing man was three times more likely to produce recorded ideas than the Company Secretary.

PLs were fairly evenly distributed amongst five of the jobs. Only in the role of Company Secretary were significantly more PLs found than we would have expected by chance. We therefore had a slight predominance of our planted idea generator in a role that required very few ideas.

The experience of having PLs in the Company Secretary role illustrates what happens when an individual has abilities that would not normally receive expression in a job. Several observers provided illuminating notes on this theme. One PL Company Secretary developed the subtle ploy of producing an idea as though it were a simple elaboration of a point made by another member (which it was not). The PL then gained the sanction of the company to record it as part of the company plan. One more universal habit of the PL Company Secretary was to work closely with the Chairman, acting like a faithful scribe, while at the same time taking advantage of the position in having the Chairman's ear to introduce a number of new ideas. These were later presented formally to the group for consideration and ratification by the Chairman. Clearly, the qualities of the person can over-ride the type of behaviour implied by the title of the job.

While we were seeking, for experimental purposes, to place one PL into each company in every course, we were precluded from comparing the fortunes of companies possessing PLs with those lacking them. When eventually we were able to make such comparison, the advantage to a company in having a PL was well supported. However, there are limits on how far creative ability can be considered as an asset.

Good ideas, as we have seen, are not always well received, especially if there are too many of them. Companies with more than one PL were found to fare no better than companies with none. Similar individual strengths offered no collective asset. The situation was comparable to that noted earlier with pure IMP teams and pure clever teams (Apollo groups). As in cooking, a surfeit of a needed ingredient ruins the dish.

The observers did admittedly describe some companies as 'very creative.' As the objective evidence that might have supported this was lacking (they did not have a higher rate of proposing than most other companies, and the ideas were not coming from the whole team) we came to the view that they were really depicting effective companies that knew how to take full advantage of good ideas. A creative company is not, any more than it is in the general business world, a pure company comprising only creative people.

After successfully proving – or so we thought – that PLs produce more ideas than other people, we followed up PL behaviour in subsequent courses and detected some remarkable ways in which the proposal rate can change. For example, in two successive courses at Henley, yielding 18 PLs, we had tried placing more than one PL in a company to see what the effect would be. Three companies were given three PLs each and two companies two PLs each. Hence there were some companies in which it would have been physically impossible for one of the PLs to get a better ranking than third in the Proposing rate. Even so, seven of the PLs finished first, four finished second, and seven finished third in the rank order of Proposing in their respective companies. None finished fourth, fifth, or sixth.

Perceived Plants: the identification of Resource Investigators

Having established this impressive start to predict creativity in a team, we nevertheless found cases where there was a consensus that some given syndicate member was a PL when our initial test scores pointed to the contrary. What could the explanation be? Was there some other type of ideas man abroad that had so far eluded the net of psychometric tests?

The individuals seen as creative who (on the basis of their test scores) were not PLs, were grouped together and their test scores were examined. The picture that emerged was that of a group of people with a definite set of characteristics in common. Whereas the PL had tended towards introversion, this group had scores markedly in the direction of extroversion. At first sight this might suggest that PLs could fall into two types, one of introverted and the other of extroverted disposition, so that they would be variants, so to speak, of the same basic model.

Further examination of the test scores and behaviour of the new group suggested that the explanation was not as simple as that. PLs (certainly good PLs) had been found to be clever, even very clever, as measured by their superior scores on the CTA. This group, however, had only average scores. On the PPQ test there were several notable construct similarities and differences between PLs and our new innovative group. Both groups tended to produce a wide range of responses. There, however, the similarities ended. PLs had a larger number than average of negative constructs (reasons for rejecting items) and their constructs were numerous in the Brain and Originality categories. Clearly, they were valuing the qualities they possessed themselves. Our new group, by contrast, had low scores in the construct categories of Brain and Originality. Instead they valued Versatility.

The 16PF recorded further differences between the two groups. Tender-mindedness, natural forthrightness, and the introverted tendencies characterizing PLs in the 16PF all vanished in the new group. In their place, the scales suggesting sociability and enthusiasm became prominent, along with scores indicative of low anxiety. In a word those perceived as PLs but not so identified on the formula could be summed up as inquisitive stable extroverts.

Having isolated this group, we now began to look more closely at their behaviour. They were, indeed, team members for whom new ideas were a focus of interest. Yet rather than standing out as originators, they were more inclined to pick up fragments of ideas from others and develop them. They were particularly adept at exploring resources outside the group. Liaison work gave them just the right opportunity to come back with some new proposition that could often transform company plans. They explored resources so well that we came to term them **Resource Investigators** (RIs).

While both RIs and PLs were seen by their colleagues as creative and therefore liable to be confused with each other, extreme examples of the type were distinct. When PLs were held to have a particularly original mind, they were almost always also regarded as oddballs and loners. However, RIs assessed as very creative usually stood out for their close involvement with people and skill in using resources. The more the RIs fulfilled their Team Role, the more they looked like managers, whereas the more PLs fulfilled their Team Role, the less they looked like any sort of manager. RIs were more easily integrated into the management team because their approach to innovation better fitted prevailing managerial axioms.

It was now plain that a team could benefit from possessing both types of innovator. Their roles were complementary. The PLs would generally sit in a corner on their own, thinking things through and sometimes coming up with some winning possibility; the RIs would ensure that no stone was left unturned and would use their special skills to find treasure in unexpected spots. If the member of the team given the Chairman role happened to be gifted, the two innovative roles would both be valued and used to advantage.

Summary

■ Numerous ideas do not make for good ideas – instead, truly creative individuals are needed.

■ A bright, creative individual was identified and called the **Plant** (PL).

■ Companies with too many PLs fared badly.

■ Another form of idea generator came to the fore, the **Resource Investigator** (RI) who brings in ideas from outside the team.

Chapter 5

Team leadership

The quickest and surest way of changing the fortunes of a firm is to replace the person at the top. This formula for success has become the stock-in-trade of those who deal with or take over ailing organisations. There is so much experience to support and reinforce this approach that the critical role of leadership in determining corporate performance can be taken for granted. Leadership is always vital and team leadership is no exception.

That being so, what are the characteristics of individuals who best lead in complex problem-solving environments where they are supported by an able set of executives? This seems a straightforward enough question. But a straightforward answer is not possible without first clarifying the question further. Is the best leader the one who is most acceptable to the group, with the personal behaviour and image that most fits what people look for in a leader? Or is the best leader the one most likely, during the tenure of office, to enable the team to reach its goals?

That important differences exist between elected and effective leaders is well attested in the research literature. Unfortunately, for the cause of democracy, elected leaders are not necessarily effective in achieving their goals. If a choice is to be made between these two types of leader, then from a management standpoint there is only one option: the effective leader has to be chosen. A more popular but less effective leader creates a fool's paradise with long-term benefits being sacrificed for short-term gain.

Experiments with company Chairmen

Taking a pragmatic view on leadership, we set about examining the records of the first 75 companies competing in the executive management exercise (EME). The method was simply to divide the companies into three groups in terms of their financial results (good, intermediate, and bad) and to scrutinize the psychometric test data of the person acting as Chairman of each group (each company had elected a Chairman). We therefore ended up with three sets of personality profiles for the leaders of the good, bad, and moderately successful companies.

As may be anticipated, successful companies had Chairmen with markedly different personalities to those which fared particularly badly. In fact, there were some sharp differences between the 16PF scores of the successful and unsuccessful Chairmen. From these data, a formula was developed that stood up well to further test and analysis in the courses that followed our initial studies. In other words, the outcome for these companies, in terms of financial results, depended in no small part on the measured personality attributes of the individual in the Chair.

Mental ability and creativity

Mental ability was naturally an important variable. Before we begin to consider the differences between successful and unsuccessful Chairmen in this respect, it is as well to reflect on what results might reasonably have been expected. Our measures included high-level reasoning ability (the Critical Thinking Appraisal [CTA]) and we had, in addition, as we have already seen, some discriminating measures of creativity based on personality dimensions. While we might believe that clever and creative Chairmen would be at an advantage, we have to bear in mind the possible differences between being a Chairman of a company in a management game and being a management leader in a firm or institution. In the latter position, long-standing experience and political skill might compensate for any limitations in intellectual or problem-solving ability.

This is not to deny the value of high mental ability as a generally useful asset in management; the point rather is to emphasize how much we expected analytical ability, judgment, and creativity to have an impact in the business games. Given the importance we discerned of such qualities in highly stable situations in which knowledge and experience grow steadily, these same assets must have even more importance in a complicated and unfamiliar management game. So we thought.

Turning these assumptions into a definite set of expectations, we could hypothesize that, in the management game, the companies with the most successful financial results would have Chairmen with high scores in mental ability and creativity; conversely, the Chairmen whose companies produced the worst results were likely to be relatively low in mental ability and creativity.

That hypothesis seemed to reflect no more than simple common sense. Indeed, every argument seemed to point in its favour. But the facts argued otherwise. Successful Chairmen were not *on average* more mentally able nor more creative than their less successful counterparts. The management game was clearly not distorting reality by overemphasizing high mental ability.

Creating a new hypothesis

Once our most promising hypothesis was out of the way, we could begin to look at what constitutes the ingredients for success. The successful Chairman was at least up to the (measured) mental ability of his colleagues; yet, not very far ahead of them. The average CTA score of all the Henley executives (including overseas members, graduates, and non-graduates) was 74. The best range in CTA score for the successful Henley Chairman lay between 75 and 80. Slightly less successful were Chairmen with scores above 80 but not exceeding 85. Much less successful were the two extreme groups: those with very high scores, or those substantially lower than the average.

A major bearing on the success rate of the Chairman was a set of personality factors derived from the personality inventory. These factors could be compounded into a formula, known as the 'successful Chairman formula'.

Personality attributes of the successful Chairman

So our successful Chairman would almost always possess a set of personality characteristics that could be defined in detail. These were made up of three main characteristics:

- A trusting nature. Successful Chairmen accepted people as they were without jealousy or suspicion;

- A strong basic dominance that to some extent counter-balanced their accepting nature; and

- A strong and morally based commitment to external goals and objectives.

Successful Chairmen also had a larger set of miscellaneous factors. They were:

■ Calm and unflappable in the face of controversy;

■ Geared towards practical realism;

■ Possessed of a basic self-discipline;

■ Naturally enthusiastic with that extrovert capacity for excitement that is known to motivate others; but also

■ Prone to detachment and distance in social relations.

One additional point of interest was that those with high scores in mental ability were, quite surprisingly, seldom appointed or elected Chairmen. It was as if the group selected as their leader one member who was not, as it were, a typical product of the group. Hartston, who was responsible for the analysis of Chairman scores, has summed up these data with a new definition of the successful Chairman: 'Someone tolerant enough always to listen to others but strong enough to reject their advice.'

In due course we were able to add to the profile of successful Chairmen by examining their construct scores on the PPQ. The successful Chairman emerged as someone who thought in very positive terms (the absence of negative words being a feature of the scores on this test); someone who used constructs that showed approval, in particular, for people who accomplished their goals and who engaged in struggle and effort; but also a liking for people who were lively and dynamic. In all these respects, the Chairmen had scores that were higher than those of their fellow team members.

Our total set of 'good Chairman' predictors played a major part in contributing to our company forecasts in the EME. If the person who took up the role of Chairman obtained a high score on our Chairman profile, we marked up the likelihood that the company would obtain a good result. Conversely, if the Chairman had a poor score on our formula, we marked down the company's chances of success.

The 'good Chairman' profile was an unexpected outcome, which was in no way affected by what we might earlier have been led to expect. It was totally the product of what the facts revealed in the search for a formula that best differentiated between those who were most effective in getting results and those who were least effective. Thus, we ended up with predictions that differed widely from those we might have made at the beginning of the endeavour.

Mental ability, communication, and control

It is worth momentarily expanding on the particularly surprising impact of mental ability. We have mentioned that particularly high or low intelligence created far less successful Chairmen than the moderate ranges. However, the relationship between mental ability and ability as Chairman was more complex than this might suggest. Chairmen with low scores in measured mental ability tended to be associated with poor company results. But these results were better than expected if they obtained good scores on the successful Chairman formula. Chairmen with very high scores in the CTA also did poorly, with few exceptions, but were less subject to the favourable influences of the formula. In other words, it seemed that Chairmen with less than desirable mental ability for the job could compensate to some extent through character attributes. However, high mental ability in a Chairman tended to overshadow the effects of personality.

We inevitably, however, sought to question why this was the case. Why should particularly high mental ability make for a worse Chairman?

With the aid of specific observations, answers began to emerge. Take the less clever Chairman. Two typical reactions were observed.

In the first case, unable to follow all the various ins and outs of the argument or the intricacy of some of the proposals that were being advanced, the Chairman was commonly inclined to opt out of proceedings, failing to exert authority or pull the group together when it faced conflicting opinions. What was seen as 'some lack of contact with members' or even 'lack of control' had its roots in a failure to comprehend the nature of the alternatives that were being put forward or to understand the arguments behind them. This Chairman often gave the impression of indecisiveness, being reluctant to make any personal stand. The group tended to lose direction and so became marked by unresolved dissension.

The other observed pattern was virtually the opposite. The Chairman hung on to control and conducted matters in a firm but oversimple fashion. Decisions would be taken without adequately exploring the options or following up either the tentative objections of dissenters or their counter-proposals. The Chairman looked for a majority view and was over-ready to turn that view into a decision at the first opportunity.

Now let us consider the clever Chairman, who would seem on the face of it to have every advantage over one short in mental ability. Yet clever Chairmen performed no better, although their results were more variable; that is to say, in a few cases results were good, in other cases indifferent, while a poor result tended to be the more common outcome.

Clever Chairmen seemed prone to get the worst of both worlds. Their inclination to exercise their skills of control, organisation, and attention to detail tended to be undermined by the distracting lure of difficult problems. Either way, they never quite fulfilled their apparent abilities. A sharp mind enabled them to keep ahead of the others but in doing so, they were liable to lose touch. While being quick to see any flaws in suggestions put forward by others, their own ideas were liable to be based on lines of argument that their team members did not always follow.

In some cases, the dominance of our clever Chairmen was so complete that their teams became, in effect, a vehicle for their own highly personalized strategies. In such instances, communication could break down completely. The intellectual authority of such Chairmen, together with the status that the position conferred on them, became enough in some instances to discourage any prospective opponents or even advocates of caution. Members failed to report facts or figures that fell within their own orbits of responsibility that might have caused inconvenience or difficulties for 'the plan'. The Chairmen would end up on their own, and not too many tears were shed by other members of the group when the plan misfired!

Chairmen with average mental ability seemed better placed. Intellectually they were on much the same wavelength as the others: if the team couldn't understand something, neither could the Chairman; what they could follow, the Chairman could too. As a result, communication operated freely in both directions. Hence, when one team member possessed evident capacities for criticism or suggestions of a superior kind, the Chairman of average intelligence was usually quick to see such talent in the team as a bonus of which use had to be made. There was no reason to feel exposed by the demonstration that one member of the team was ahead of the rest of the field. The Chairman's decisiveness showed in knowing whom to back.

The ideal Chairman

We were gradually able, therefore, to sketch an ideal Chairman by combining an appreciation of their mental ability with their specific personality attributes. In terms of the data we had about these ideal figures, they seemed to possess a set of perfectly commonplace characteristics, yet characteristics that were put together in an uncommon way. So unusual was the combination that, in fact, we had considerable difficulty in finding individuals who displayed all the combinations of attributes that our empirical study of the effective Chairman had revealed. When our ideal Chairmen did emerge, they still looked like ordinary team members in some respects. Yet their results could be outstanding.

It is quite difficult to identify individuals with this gift, for it belongs to some deceptively ordinary people. The ability to act well in the Chair is in itself a common accomplishment. But the value of this skill falls a good deal short of the ability to obtain a first-rate result from a team over which a Chairman presides.

Implications of results

At this point, a certain amount of rationalization would not come amiss. Why, we may ask ourselves, should such individuals prove so successful, when their personal qualities and abilities are hardly in line with those that scrutiny of the game would suggest as a desirable specification for winning it?

To answer this question, we have to consider the implications of the scores that did mark out our successful Chairman. These suggest that the person at the helm was not the individual who was personally showing his flock the way through the maze of difficult problems that beset a company in this complex exercise. In the last chapter, we identified just the individual with the creative flair who might have done this. We called those team members Plants (PLs). Evidently, a PL acting as Chairman would have conferred less advantage on the company than the sort of person that our pragmatic study has revealed.

What then are the real assets of this team leader? In a word, the ideal Chairman looks like a manager – an individual who knows how to use resources, who is singularly adaptive when it comes to people but who never loses grip on a situation. Furthermore, good Chairmen retain their ability to reach their own judgment based on their assessment of what is needed in practice.

While this ideal Chairman specification seems also to fit that of a manager, the two should not be seen as coinciding. Not all managers are ideal leaders of teams. Some managers barely conceal their impatience with teams, with committees, or indeed with anything that smacks of group leadership. Other managers possess such singular talents that their staff are essentially only supportive: the dominant managers make the decisions and give their staff explicit directives so that quite senior members of their team still act as though under day-to-day instruction – even when the manager is out of the country.

Our Chairman-managers seem very different. That they had a distinctive style of managing was apparent from the reports that the observers in the exercise were able to furnish. The successful Chairmen were not all that dissimilar from other team members, but they did stand out as individuals who carried the respect of others. Their interventions were most apparent at critical points in the exercise. Then they would be the figure in command, striving to pull the whole thing together. Chairmen would also never allow meetings to get out of hand. At moments of dissension, they were ever ready to impart a sense of direction and purpose.

From Chairman to Co-ordinator

What only gradually became apparent, therefore, was that the effective chairman reflected personality rather than rank. Instead, our Chairmen functioned best when overseeing the exercise, clarifying where the team was going, and canvassing the opinions of others rather than making decisions alone. They were also adept at ensuring that the members of the team played their roles effectively and did not attempt to complete all tasks alone. Thus our Chairmen were not the traditional company manager who had automatic ascendancy. Instead, they were calm, confident and mature individuals possessed of a good degree of emotional intelligence and conscientiousness who kept others working together by dint of their good understanding of objectives and dynamics. In time, we came to rename the Chairman Team Role to reflect effective behaviour in the Chair rather than their rank.

So Chairman became the Team Role **Co ordinator** (CO) – another advantage being that COs could be female as well as male. CO behaviour can be exhibited in almost any responsible job. The Company Secretary might be a fine CO and achieve good results by working alongside and through the official Chairman, for example. However, teams where the principle CO was acting as Chairman fared better because the individual who was most able at overseeing and clarifying the goals of the team was free to do so and not bound by the requirements of another field. Such individuals were able to make the most of their broad outlook, and to fulfil their natural role without conflicting with another apparent leadership figure.

CASE STUDY – A NON-DOMINANT CHAIRMAN

Edna Mainstay was a practical, sensible lady of character with no pretensions to intellectual distinction, holding a very senior appointment in her profession. When we composed the team of which she was a member, we included a brilliant but difficult person along with a lively communicator who looked as though he would get around well outside the group and ensure that the group would not lose touch with its environment. An observer recorded with copious notes all that happened. Edna was made Chairman and the company ended up with a final result well ahead of its other seven rivals in the field. Throughout the exercise, the right people seemed to do the right thing at the right time.

The observer gave no credit to the Chairman for her control over the proceedings, merely noting that she did not take a leading role. The two leading members of the group took a different view, praising her rather than each other or themselves. Skill in consultation, delegation of work, and firmness of decisions all earned high marks. Edna eventually joined one of our early seminars on management team building and so took part in Teamopoly. As the teams consisted of only four members, the role of Chairman is often left vacant and the members operate instead as a closely knit group. In this instance, however, she was made Chairman in a formal sense. Again she was inconspicuous in the way in which she performed her duties but each team member found himself naturally cast in the right job. Everything fell into place and the team won. 'In my professional role I am used to working with consultants on committees,' our Chairman declared, 'and I think I know how to get the best out of them.'

Edna's success was also significant in what was, at the time, a very male-dominated environment. High-level managers who happened to be female were very few and far between during the 1970s, but the appreciation of Edna's colleagues showed that the arena of management and management exercises could suit women just as well as men. Perhaps it is interesting that she was accepted as the team's Chairman precisely because she did not attempt to dominate, but instead used her skills in a subtle way.

A different sort of leader

The management team-building seminars that we set up after our experience with experimental companies at Henley attracted a new range of people, including some in very senior positions. Group Personnel Managers for multinational organisations were well represented and there were a fair number of successful Managing Directors who were now interested in finding executive teams to spawn subsidiary companies.

Amongst this senior group we expected to find a good proportion of men with the typical Chairman profile. We were surprised to find that this was not so. We had developed a leadership formula through painstaking research, which we had put to the test by giving it a key position in our forecasting formulae. These forecasts had stood up to the test well, admittedly not in all cases, but to an extent that gave grounds for belief that we were well and truly on the right track. Now we were faced with the surprising phenomenon that a substantial class of known leaders did not accord with the general shape of the profile. They did not even resemble them. What then was the explanation?

The immediate thought was that some differences existed between artificial team games of the sort that are practised in management training establishments and the reality of team leadership in the business and institutional world. If this were so, we could have been acting on the wrong specification, recommending to industry men who might make good captains for teams in artificial games but who might fall down on the job in leading real teams. This seemed an obvious danger. What was needed was evidence to either confirm or dismiss this possibility.

The first question was whether our effective Chairmen performed well as team leaders in the organisations from which they came. The evidence that came our way was necessarily personalized and informal. We were looking especially for qualitative information: did they have any characteristic management style? Where did their personal strengths lie? Were their strengths in the business world the same as we had identified in our exercise?

We did not get hold of all the information that we would have liked, but the Henley grapevine and system of personal contacts can work remarkably well when the need arises. The message that came back seemed unequivocal enough. The abilities that these individuals possessed in their jobs seemed to lie very much in the qualities of leadership that we had already attributed to them in the training exercise. So at least, our conclusions about them in terms of behaviour were accurate when it came to real-world performance.

It was then useful to examine placements made in industry using the good CO profile. Had our recommended candidates become good managers in practice?

By now we had carried out a good deal of work in industry in using the strategies. Techniques of placing or managing candidates with the CO profile had stood up well. In the field of computer applications, several field experiences had proved rewarding. Leaders of project teams had been appointed on the basis of CO scores rather than on the basis of experience and seniority, and favourable outcomes had been reported.

CASE STUDY – A CO-ORDINATOR'S SUCCESS IN A REAL-LIFE PROJECT TEAM

Another notable experience had been with a product development team in plastics. This team had not met with much commercial success. By chance the Project Leader was transferred to another job. A new man moved in whose personal knowledge of the technology was rather scant and who was not high on CO characteristics. This did not make him an obvious choice to oversee the project. As it happened, the No. 2 in the team had an impressive CO score. The new manager seized on the opportunity and said 'Why don't you take the Chair? I would far prefer to act as the backbench MP and direct myself to criticisms of the front bench.' This somewhat unorthodox procedure was set in motion. The whole experiment worked well. The re-formed project team soon made a major impact in its chosen business field and the effectiveness of its management teamwork was hailed as the cornerstone of its achievement.

None of this evidence suggested that our team leader profile was missing the mark. So we had to search for other explanations of why so many senior managers were different from the team leaders highlighted by our experiments.

Shapers

The explanation that now seemed likely was that a good proportion of the proven managers at our seminars belonged to a distinctive group of effective leaders, who tended to thrive in (and to be thrown up by) particular types of environment. If this was so, there was the prospect of a cluster of managerial characteristics that had not previously come to light in our studies. It was now necessary to take these into account.

The problem was that, in the personal counselling session, which we afforded each seminar participant, we always had something to say about how a given individual's strengths and abilities might be used to advantage in contributing to the collective effort of the team. For these unexpected leaders, we had little to offer that was constructive. We could not equate these successful leaders with any of the Team Roles we had thus far found essential or desirable for the success of a team (although other Team Roles also came to light in the later stages of the investigation). For the moment, the role and contribution of these 'leaders' was an uncertain one.

Our personality measures gave us some initial characteristics to help us identify these proven managers, and these characteristics were backed up by their behaviour in the exercises. They were extroverts abounding in nervous energy and actuated by the need for achievement.

In many ways, these team members were the antithesis of a person you might expect to make a good team player. They challenged, argued, and disagreed. Rather than allowing events and people to dictate their actions, they would drive actions in their own desired direction.

It was this that led us to christen these people **Shapers** (SHs). There were also other qualities associated with this type of behaviour – ones that on first glance would seem to make them unlikely to be successful in a team environment. They were impatient and easily frustrated. Their proneness to aggression would produce a reciprocal reaction from other team members; yet, they would respond with remarkably good humour and resilience as though they thoroughly enjoyed a battle.

Our SHs were also highly competitive. Winning was the name of the game as far as they were concerned, and learning was very much the secondary objective. If their team was doing poorly, they would question the rules or the fairness of the umpiring; yet, they had no hesitation in pursuing their goals by illicit means. On one notable occasion in Cambridge, one of the teams possessed a strong SH. Seeing the potential for their own team to fail, they waited until a rival company was out of the room and set fire to their paperwork plans.

Once our exercises had ended and our SHs could put aside their concentration on winning, a new and sudden interest erupted in the lessons for the future, in the way in which the message could be put across back at the firm. The more poorly their companies had performed, the greater the intensity of their interest, in spite of their smarting at the mistakes that they (or more usually in their eyes, another member of the team) had made.

Experimenting with Shaper teams

In due course, we formed companies of SHs in our Teamopoly exercises for the purpose of learning something more about them. They never failed to illustrate for our seminar participants how the character of a company can be moulded by the team types that are enrolled. Whether they did well or poorly, they always created uproar. In a seminar we ran in Canberra for government officials, one company of SHs spent a good deal of time successfully disrupting other rival companies by both legitimate and illegitimate means.

While such behaviour by government officials surprised us at the time, it was mild in comparison with our last experience in Melbourne. There a team of SHs, which had sunk into a bad last place through extravagant overbidding and a failure to co-ordinate their plans effectively, resorted to desperate antics. These included securing a live pistol with a view to kidnapping the auctioneer (failing, as it happened, through a change of venue), stealing money from the bank, followed by a demand for money for 'information received', and holding a lady member of the winning team hostage by brute force for the purpose of ransom. This tomfoolery helped dispel the tension caused by not winning and provided an alternative and enjoyable form of substitute achievement.

With infamous conduct being a common feature of such companies, my colleague, Neil Stucley, decided that a new term was needed to sum up such SH antics. He invented a new collective noun: 'a shockery of Shapers'.

But back to our methods and findings for these teams. We chose to select our teams of SHs principally based on the feedback of their team members. We had touched on such a method in identifying our PLs, and these methods were the early basis for a real Team Role Inventory, which is now one of the most widely used inventories across the globe. But the formal development of the inventory occurred at a later stage, so we will leave its details until that point.

At this stage, we simply used our inventory to indicate those who appeared to be SHs. We then went back to their test scores so that for forecasting purposes we could establish what type of test profile made a SH. Statistically, the data gave the highest loadings on apprehension, suspicion, proneness to frustration, and sociability. Additionally, the SH was opportunistic rather than conscientious, tough-minded, emotional, but free from shyness and social timidity. All this suggested a tough anxious extrovert, an individual prone to over-react to disappointments or annoyances, but resilient, fearless, and unflinching with people.

As we gained experience in introducing SHs individually into teams and in composing teams consisting entirely of SHs, we began to appreciate that SHs had very definite pros and cons. There was never any doubt that an SH-led group would be galvanized into action. If a group was prone to complacency or inaction, the presence of an SH restored the balance so that performance improved. However, an

SH was usually a disruptive force in a well-balanced group, especially one led by someone with a typical CO profile.

Collectively, SHs did not have the best record as far as results were concerned. A team of SHs tended to generate its own culture, often achieving a high work rate, being quick to explore all possible avenues of approach and abandoning any that did not look rewarding. However, they seldom liked working with each other and it was clear that a team built on their lines would sooner or later run into difficulties. In spite of a great deal of positive goal-directed activity, the damaging consequences of in-fighting tended to lead to poor results. In these cases, the combination of aggravation and failure was too much to bear. People were only too ready to choose a scapegoat and testify to their sins, giving full vent to their indignation.

Co-ordinators and Shapers as contrasting leaders

The effective CO and SH profiles gave us two approaches to leadership. The most reliable results, both in our own training exercises and in the industrial assignments on which we worked, were yielded by the effective CO profile. Yet known leaders outside Henley were more likely to display the SH profile. How could we explain this seeming paradox?

There seemed two likely levels of explanation. One was that the highly active, dynamic, restless manager may be less attracted to a 10-week interlude in management education in a quiet beauty spot of the Chilterns than in presenting himself for a 3-day seminar where there was the prospect that he might pick up something useful quickly. Certainly, we detected over the years a population difference, with a good supply of COs and a scarcity of SHs at Henley against an abundance of SHs and a dearth of COs in our seminars.

Another part of the explanation must relate to a basic bifurcation to which the whole field of leadership is subject. There is a strong situational difference between leading a group in a directive way and marshalling the resources of a team, especially where that team is well equipped to tackle a complex set of inter-relating problems.

Many organisations present some sort of dilemma where the leadership is concerned and the question of complexity lies at the very heart of the matter. As well as complexity of problems there is another type – political complexity. Where issues require concerted action by people operating at different levels and subject to their own, sometimes conflicting, set of rules, regulations, and constraints, inertia almost inevitably sets in. In dealing with the stagnation that this political complexity generates, the SH thrives. The SH is effective in gingering up slow-moving systems or even in changing the way in which they function so that certain ends may be achieved. Provided the SH is right in any analysis made of the needs of the situation, he or she makes such a positive impact that promotion is guaranteed.

Different styles of leadership in different situations

One key point that became clear was the difference in success between different roles in the two different games. In the EME, COs who fulfilled the Chairman role were almost always successful, where the blunter, more dynamic, and less calm SH would rarely be. Yet in Teamopoly, those SHs who found themselves in the role of Chairman generally did well. Our modified Monopoly game seemed more suited to their leadership talents than did the EME.

The difference lay in the requirements of the two. Where in EME effective planning and co-ordination were absolutely vital, in Teamopoly there were many ways in which action and initiative were rewarded. Planning and co-ordination still played a part but had a less all-embracing influence than in the EME. The shorter time frame, the greater the opportunity to have crises to be dealt with, and the more restrictive methods of receiving property, all played more to the strengths of the SH.

We had designed Teamopoly so as to incorporate, as we saw it, the main body of skills that are crucial in top management. One avenue was open for the sort of skills that SHs possess. By being themselves and using their natural drive, persistence, and high-pressure negotiating skills to advantage, they were capable of outmanoeuvring the other companies. But where this outmanoeuvring failed, they had less to fall back on than the calm COs with their good sense of overview and priorities.

Just as there are horses for courses, so there are leaders for teams. We have established two archetypal leaders, one combining skilful use of the reserves of the group with the effective control of team members (the CO) and the other an instigator of action (the SH), the latter of the two as often as not succeeding by dragging the team along after. Clearly, the nature of the challenge and the characteristics of the team members have a bearing on which of these two leaders best suits a situation.

Apollo Chairmen

While CO and SH team leaders between them can cover most situations, there was one more team leader that our studies finally managed to reveal. This was the leader best fitted to cope with a team comprising individuals of very high mental ability, typically an Apollo team as we christened it in Chapter 2. This team was susceptible to under-achievement: their corporate capability fell short of the standards expected by reason of the individual abilities of those who formed the team.

While such teams tended to perform poorly even in comparison with run-of-the-mill companies, there were some instances where Apollo teams encountered the usual difficulties but overcame them to finish well. In these instances, the Chairman appeared to play an important part. We therefore became interested in successful Apollo Chairmen. Were they closer to the CO or the SH type of leader?

In one respect, successful Apollo Chairmen were like most successful CO Chairmen by being slightly, and only slightly, cleverer than the groups over which they were presiding. In practice, of course, this made them cleverer than the general run of successful Chairmen since Apollos were cleverer than other groups.

In other respects, Apollo Chairmen were unlike our COs, showing a number of SH traits. Yet they were not really SHs, for they lacked the SH's restless desire to lead from the front. The main distinguishing feature of the Apollo Chairmen, as revealed by analysis of their psychometric test scores, was a marked rise in those personality scores suggesting suspicion and scepticism compensated by a small fall in dominance and a move away from the concern for practical matters towards an interest in broad essentials.

These results made sense to us, especially when they were supplemented by observer reports that indicated the successful Apollo Chairman's style of operation. The essential behavioural difference between the CO and the Apollo Chairman lies in the approach to the group. The CO is adept at drawing out the potential of the group; recognizes and encourages all those aspects of talent and ability that must be cultivated if the team is to achieve its objectives; and has a talent for spotting and developing the creative flair of the individual who would normally lie submerged in the group. The Apollo Chairman, however, is less of a searcher after talent; rather this type of Chairman is a tough, discriminating person who can hold ground in any company, and yet never dominates.

Three leaders

Having identified three distinct forms of leader that seemed to bring about successful results, we felt fairly confident that with the aid of our psychometric test instruments we could select them. One is suited for the balanced team that, due to its Team Role distribution, possesses at a number of levels the potential for coping with complex multidimensional problems; another fits the team that has the established capability to do well but which faces obstacles that are either internal or external; and the third type is appropriate to the 'think tank' type of team. The CO, the SH and the Apollo Chairman are the leaders who correspond with and are appropriate to these teams between which we find it useful to distinguish.

What can be said about team leaders who cannot be equated with any one of our three types and whose personal qualities and characteristics are altogether different? Some have long established and proven competence as team leaders or as formal Chairmen of committees.

Our early investigations suggested a process of learning. We identified the possibility that a person who had proved worth in some part of the managerial orbit often endeavoured to become effective in other fields towards which he or she possessed no natural aptitude. The very challenge was a motivating factor. A manager gifted with high intelligence and a capacity for balanced judgment may have also been so shy and self-effacing (on the evidence of test data) that it was difficult to conceive of discharging some of the responsibilities associated with high office. Yet the manager rose to the occasion, acting in exactly the way that was required. This performance was atypical of the manager's normal, natural behaviour. Provided not too many calls were made upon such managers to act in this way, they survived and may even at times have distinguished themselves. But if they became overloaded with demands that pressurized them away from their natural and preferred role, they began frequently to look around for another job or choose early retirement.

This theory accounted for some, but not all of our successful managers. Others seemed to operate on a much more consistent level, but in a way that was very different from our assumed three styles of leadership. It is only after many years of first-hand experience that the reason behind these anomalous individuals became really apparent.

The answer was, strangely, self-awareness. Those managers who had apparently non-managerial Team Role types, such as Implementers, succeeded by being aware of their strengths and weaknesses. They applied their strengths well, and managed their weaknesses, usually by allying themselves with those of a very different turn of mind who could compensate where they lacked. It became clear that an individual with any Team Roles (or combination thereof) could in fact become some form of manager, provided they had the awareness and intuition to make the most of what they had.

Whether an individual manager who is not typically a team leader possesses the talent and readiness to lead a team depends on whether he or she can develop over time a convincing style of leadership that suits the essential personality. But it must also depend on the extent of the fit between the leader and the team. How far does he or she supply something that the team lacks? Here we have to learn more about what a good team needs and about the range of contributions from the team members that keep it in balance.

Summary

■ The most effective team leaders were not the highest scorers in mental ability.

■ A profile was created that matched most successful team leaders and given the name **Co-ordinator** (CO).

■ Other team leaders, less calm and more driven, proved successful at times and these were termed **Shapers** (SHs).

■ There were variations in leadership that met the needs of particular situations, as in the case of the Apollo team of "experts".

Chapter 6

Other key
team roles

By now, we have established some of the primary characteristics for successful teams.

It might be thought that the task of sorting out the best ideas should fall to the team leader. Yet this is not the case. As we have seen earlier, the team leader is likely to have mental abilities no higher than the average, which does not equip him or her for evaluating or analysing the ideas of Plants (PLs) or Resource Investigators (RIs). The evaluation of competing proposals calls for a person who possesses a high level of mental ability combined with disinterested detachment. From time to time such a person came to the fore at critical moments in the EME to act in this new and distinctive role. We christened this individual the **Monitor Evaluator** (ME).

The Monitor Evaluator

In certain cases, observers recorded the emergence of one member of a team who, as often as not, had not figured very prominently until a crucial decision had to be made. A brilliant PL or an enthusiastic RI may be valued members of a group but they are seldom the best people to judge the merits of any idea they are putting forward. Nor are most other members of a team. In one way or another they are too respectful or too awestruck by a particular member – or they lack the sharpness of mind to find the critical flaw in an argument.

The newcomer was able to fill the void. Intellectually, MEs were the only people who could hold their own in debate with PLs, and could cause the PLs to change standpoint and retain their respect in so doing.

By examining the test scores of those individuals who filled this role and by observing their behaviour closely, we were able to provide a detailed picture of what the ME looked like and so built up a role specification. In the first place the ME was a high scorer in the Critical Thinking Appraisal, doing especially well in the final section of the test that deals with controversial arguments. In other words the soundness of the ME's judgements was not disturbed by the introduction of emotionally loaded material designed to play on prejudice.

MEs also had very distinct personality characteristics. They emerged from the test as serious-minded, prudent individuals with a built-in immunity from enthusiasm. They would be slow in making up their minds, always preferring to think things over. Their real asset was the capacity for making shrewd judgements that took all factors into account. Our MEs would take pride in never being wrong but they would stake no claim towards originality or imagination.

On the construct analysis of the PPQ, MEs emerged as having a significantly low achievement orientation, meaning in essence a low sense of drive. In due course we came to realize that this apparent failing conferred an advantage. Drive interferes with judgement: true impartiality is best served by a total lack of commitment.

There are, of course, certain problems associated with this type of profile, as there is with all of the team roles. In the case of the ME, their principal problem is one of presentation. They tend to come across as dry, boring, and sometimes overcritical. They furthermore will, by necessity, lack charisma and enthusiasm. Many people are surprised that they ever become managers.

The intellectual and decision-making abilities of good MEs are impressive, however. There are scores of them who occupy strategic posts in commerce or industry and thrive in high-level appointments, especially in Head Offices. In some jobs success or failure hinges on a relatively small number of big crunch decisions. This is the ideal territory for an ME, for the individual who is never wrong is the one who scores in the end.

CASE STUDY – MONITOR EVALUATOR MANAGEMENT IN A FIRM

The ME style of managing was brought home to me in a personal way in my experiences in a long-established institution which I used to visit regularly in the City of London. The purpose of my visits was to introduce new methods of handling the operational side of the business. These were being introduced into a somewhat conservative environment with a traditional way of doing things.

The manager, known as the master, had the cautious qualities and characteristics that might have been expected in someone holding that particular office. This did not detract from the fact that he was a man of high ability with a deep and extensive knowledge of his subject, ever conscious of the need for change, if a rational case for change could ever be made out.

The agenda for our meetings was strictly limited. We usually had only one item to discuss. The single problem would be the one we had both prepared for before we met. Analysis of the problem would usually leave us with about four options on which we could proceed once we had committed ourselves to a particular line of action.

We would meet first thing in the morning. Each option would be discussed as though it had equal merits with any other. We would ruminate over each proposal. If there were any conceivable objections to a new proposal, we would take them on board. Yet even the least promising option at that stage could not be dismissed out of hand.

In due course we would run short of arguments and counter-arguments and conversation would lag almost to nothing. No telephone calls or casual callers would interrupt the silence for – unlike most managers – the master would ensure that we were free from disturbance. Occasionally a knock would be heard at the door but this was never answered. A queue of people sometimes formed outside, quaintly hopeful of eventual admission, past which only one privileged person would proceed unchallenged – the tea lady whose smiling maternal presence was guaranteed for mid-morning. After her departure we would be back to re-examining the four options to which perhaps a fifth might be added before being eventually withdrawn.

A long-anticipated lunch would at last provide a change of topic, which then became as open-ended and as far-ranging as the earlier conversation had been restricted. After this one-hour intermission we would return to our office for a new look, if that were possible, at the familiar options. By mid-afternoon a final decision would be reached and the necessary steps taken to turn that decision into action. The office door would then be opened and the patience of any remaining morning visitors would be rewarded.

A phenomenon is sometimes better comprehended by considering its opposite. An ME style of management is exactly what seat-of-the-pants management is not. Seat-of-the-pants management generates for any given period of time a relatively large number of decisions; these are mainly of the instantly made variety. Anyone who manages in this style cheerfully takes the risk that some are likely to be wide of the mark. By contrast, ME management over the same stretch of time will generate very few decisions. But it is almost certain that any decisions will be the right ones.

While the personality characteristics of MEs do not suggest typical team players, MEs nevertheless often fit very comfortably into a team. This is especially the case if their role is clear both to them and to others. The slowness of teams in moving to decisions is not a feature that will aggravate them. Indeed, such slow movement provides them with an opportunity to come into their element.

Ideally the ME, rather than the CO, should be the arbiter of decision-making within the group. The more numerous the suggestions on offer, and the more complex the decision-making process, the more important this role becomes.

The Teamworker

Inevitably, with such important but fine distinctions between the Team Roles of members, many hazards arise in getting a group of diverse people to work together effectively – even with a really capable CO. For one thing, people are often disinclined to accept the Team Role for which they may be best fitted. Somebody else's Team Role presents irresistible attractions.

This can create difficulties when those with a real ability in an area are not as assertive as others in a team. In the case of an ME, the natural and talented arbiter is unlikely to be the most forthcoming, likely as they are to be slow-moving. They are likely, as a result, to be squeezed out of a potential contribution by more ebullient individuals, all anxious to put on record their own verdicts and judgements. In the same way, a shy but highly creative PL may be shut out by others of lower ability, anxious to give full rein to their own ideas. The danger in many groups is that individuals strive competitively to make their voice heard on any matter that comes up; no one is interested in heeding anyone else, and still less in considering that others may have an ability in the area where they are asserting their views.

While members of some companies were very prone to display this behaviour, there were occasions when a single member would stand out as the exception. Occasionally such a person would save the day. A helpful intervention would avert potential friction and enable difficult characters in the team to use their skills to positive ends. Anyone who possesses a talent of this sort has a particular part to play in making a team successful, especially when it contains one or more individuals with outstanding talent but who are unable to work with colleagues.

In due course we came to recognize the need for a Team Role in this area. We enlisted the help of our observers in the EME to identify individuals who had skill in listening to others and coping with awkward people, and who exercised a favourable influence on team spirit by placing group objectives above self-interest.

One sample of people who fell into this Team Role – on which we soon conferred the title of **Teamworker** (TW) – yielded a set of revealing psychometric test scores. The TW was found to have the sociability scores commonly associated with extroverts but the low dominance scores of the introverts. The TW emerged as a trusting and sensitive personality with constructs on the PPQ test showing a strong interest in people, especially in human interaction and communication.

Some managers expressed disappointment when they found themselves dubbed TW on the basis of the various methods of assessment that we developed to establish a person's ideal Team Role. It was hard for them to envisage a TW in anything other than a support job.

There was genuine surprise that TWs were not uncommonly found amongst top managers on the evidence of both their psychometric test scores and their behaviour as perceived by colleagues. Environments which are dominated by SH line managers can create a climate in which the diplomatic and perceptive skills of the TW become real assets, especially where an authoritarian and conflict-ridden managerial regime has run into trouble. Thus the TW manager, seen as a threat to no one and as a benefit to the group interest, is favoured by peers as the one they would be prepared to serve under most willingly.

CASE STUDY – A TEAMWORKER MANAGER

I encountered a good example of a top-level TW manager in the industrial world. This individual was also, as it happened, the first person to invite me to help in reconstructing an industrial team. It is entirely in keeping that such a person should have been interested in pioneering teamwork. Concern for team-members, colleagues, or employees is a characteristic of the TW.

As a director in charge of research and development in a large industrial organisation, he was beset with a familiar problem: an occasional project would produce an immense commercial pay-off, while many projects had very little to show for the large sums of

Continued

money they consumed. That was held as being largely unavoidable. What was disturbing, however, was to find a project team that had a long history of solid work and investigation being overtaken by a smaller firm that had obviously invested far less in the same project area. There seemed a possibility here of some imbalance or weakness in the long-established project team.

And so it proved. Over a period of time the director made steady headway in a very controversial area. He moved his personnel around in such a way that their weaknesses were not exposed and they contributed from their strengths. His personal management style was non-provocative, non-threatening, but persuasive. In meetings with his managers he talked a good deal less than is normally expected of a 'boss' and listened more. Other managers followed suit by talking less too. Less noise and more messages characterized any meeting at which he presided.

His style was distinctive too in informal situations. The director was always being consulted by others. He was regarded as a man with rare skills, as a coach and tutor by graduates at junior levels of the hierarchy. At the most senior levels he was a confidant of one or two managers commonly regarded as unapproachable. In consequence he was seen as a man of influence. The position that he had reached clearly owed much to the way in which he had perfected his particular style of managing to take account both of the needs of situations and his own personality and capabilities.

TWs seem to have a lubricating effect on teams. Morale is better and people seem to co-operate more when they are present. Some groups are bound to contain awkward members. When that occurs, one or more TWs can exercise a subtle influence in averting potential conflict, and can help make the task of whoever is formally chairing the meeting a much easier one.

Completer Finisher

So far, we have found the range of useful people in teams to cover seven Team Roles. To these an eighth can be added, the **Completer Finisher** (CF). The ability to take work and perfect it is a quality that is important in any undertaking. Whilst Implementers (IMPs) will produce large volumes of work with great efficiency, CFs will check it all for errors, ensuring that nothing is sent out or signed off until it is perfect. They are driven by an inward anxiety to get all things right, and can paradoxically find finishing a task off very difficult: it will never seem to be quite perfect enough. They finish in terms of adding polish to a job, rather than seeing everything through to conclusion swiftly.

Whilst other members of a team would attempt to proof-read or double-check work, it was found that those without the real anxiety to ensure perfection would never perform this task as thoroughly.

Unfortunately this personal quality of perfectionism is one that seems to be in short supply. We found few strong CFs amongst our tested managers. To add to the difficulty, the quality of perfectionism is not easy to discern when a candidate is being interviewed as part of the selection process for jobs. Enthusiasm to get things moving may easily be detected but the ability to follow through properly once started is much less evident. Furthermore, when it comes to interview, the anxiety that characterizes CFs is unlikely to make for a good interview candidate. Interviewers must work hard to draw them out, where a talkative RI or a calm and confident CO would have few troubles.

CASE STUDY – A LACK OF COMPLETER FINISHER

If a Team Role can be best understood by considering those human deficiencies which create a need for it, then a good example came our way when we had occasion to run a graduate induction programme for a national airline. We had been asked to introduce the concept of management Team Roles to 16 graduates recruited from an original field of 300 screened applicants. Since the applicants had been submitted to a battery of tests including measures of mental ability, the 16 selected candidates showed themselves to be impressively bright during the seminar, as might be expected. The tests we gave them were however related to personal characteristics indicating likely affinity or lack of affinity for the given Team Roles.

My colleague Bill Hartston and I then interviewed each of the course members to discuss the implications of their test scores. Some of the course members were low in the CF Team Role and this was particularly so in the case of one young lady. When Hartston discreetly pointed out the facts to her, she hastened to agree, observing, 'I wonder if that would tie up with the fact that I have been knitting myself a jumper for nine years and it is still unfinished.'

What our studies had discovered was that poor finishing qualities were associated with individuals who tended to have a cavalier attitude to detail and a low regard for obligations. Whole teams made up of such individuals almost invariably failed. The lack of a CF emerged as a common reason for teams that looked to be within certain grasp of their goals – and then fell at the very last hurdle.

It was a typical experience in the Henley management game to find small computational errors upsetting a well-conceived operational strategy. In the exercise that played a central part in the team-building seminars, companies sometimes missed key auctions and tenders by late attendance, often of no more than a few vital seconds. If a battle was lost for a horse and the horse for a shoe and the shoe for a nail, then the old proverb seemed to have lost none of its relevance. Small mishaps can spell grave misfortune. Attention to detail is not a trivial matter. Someone with a capacity for relentless follow-through is a real asset in any team.

Our experiences had many counterparts in the industrial world, especially in the launching of new products and models. Often a product is well conceived but fails to establish its share in the market due to some early reverse from which it never recovers. The launching team may be well equipped with enthusiasts amongst its designers, marketeers, and salesmen, most of whom look forward eagerly to D-day. What tends to be lacking is someone prepared to hold things back until all the necessary tests, checks, and safeguards have been completed and the product can be announced as truly ready to go. Sometimes the tests reveal that the product is not in fact a runner and should be scrapped or redesigned. Market research or independent laboratory testing may provide the unwelcome news – but news that may save a company from ruin.

CASE STUDY – THE NEED FOR A COMPLETER FINISHER IN INDUSTRY

A good illustration of the need for a CF arose during a period in which I ran seminars on Total Quality Control for the British Institute of Management. On their behalf I published a paper on Quality Calamities. During the course of this work I was able to obtain information on 121 Quality Calamities (defined as simple quality-related incidents that resulted in a large financial loss).

The underlying causes of those calamities were studied and at the forefront came lack of proving (whether of new designs, materials, or processes). This accounted for 36% of all cases.

A typical instance of a large calamity was provided by a company manufacturing rubber thread by a continuous process which involved extruding latex into acetic acid and drawing it through a casing oven to emerge, in its finished state, ready for covering with yarn. As the price of natural rubber increased, the company found itself compelled to search for alternative materials.

An American company, with which it had associations, had just launched a new synthetic rubber thread. This was a good deal cheaper. Moreover, advantages were claimed for some of its physical properties. Negotiations began and the British team soon committed itself to take up the licence for the UK. Production was switched from natural to synthetic rubber thread and customers were persuaded that they would enjoy a number of benefits. In their haste to accept the deal, the British company omitted to submit the new rubber to the exhaustive range of tests that their well-equipped technical laboratory could provide. One of these tests covered accelerated ageing. Once the new rubber was in use, it was found to have poor ageing properties which made it unsuitable for its main market outlet. Claims from customers for damages resulted and in the end the whole venture had to be abandoned with consequential losses estimated to exceed two million pounds. There had been nothing at fault with the detailed technical information furnished by the American company. It was just that one physical property was not mentioned. No one in the British management team had thought it worthwhile to submit the product to a total check.

It requires a manager with a particular attitude of mind to plan ahead, to ensure that nothing is overlooked and that all detailed plans have been completed to satisfaction. We therefore set out to look for CF managers who displayed this particular facility in our experimental situations. They were not easy to find, for many managers confessed to losing interest in a new idea once all the exciting new features had been explored. Yet success is seldom easily earned and a certain sense of perfectionism is indispensable for achievement. In time we reached the view that CF managers tended to fight shy of training and education courses – but they were not uncommon when one got into the heart of successful enterprises.

By taking good examples of the CF type of manager, we were able to establish a set of psychometric test scores which matched the behaviour patterns we observed. What these scores tended to reveal was that CF managers, though prone to anxiety, were high in self-control and self-discipline. Their peers in their syndicates and companies seldom saw them as anxious, even veering in the other direction and regarding them as calm and unflappable. All anxiety was internalized.

CF managers also tended to be introverted rather than extroverted. They seemed to look for and absorb stress, although it would take its toll sometimes in physical terms. In due course we came to interpret an ulcer as a promising sign of the ideal CF manager! On the construct analysis of the PPQ the CF manager tended to favour steady effort, survival, consistency, and was less interested in the glamour of spectacular success.

The CF style of management, along with IMP and TW styles, tends to be underrated and managers need persuasion that this style is not uncommon amongst successful top managers. Inevitably distortions arise in the public mind about the characteristics of top management.

Managers in the news tend naturally to be those of more flamboyant disposition and are therefore accepted as generally representative of the genus. But behind the scenes many top managers differ from the stereotype of the big businessman. Their success is founded on the more sterling qualities of character and discipline that underline their capacity for hard, effective work.

Time is never wasted when CF managers are in place. Ideally, their qualities need to be widened and socialized. They are concerned not merely with perfecting for their own needs, but for the wider group. Good finishing is a valued art and the person who makes his or her mark in this area is quickly recognized and appreciated by his colleagues.

Conclusion

The useful people to have in teams are those who possess strengths or characteristics which serve a need without duplicating those already there. Teams are a question of balance. What is needed is not well-balanced individuals but individuals who balance well with one another. In that way, human frailties can be underpinned and strengths used to full advantage.

Summary

■ The ideas of Plants (PLs) and Resource Investigators (RIs) require evaluation by a logical, objective individual we called the **Monitor Evaluator** (ME).

■ Difficult personal situations also require particular diplomatic abilities, fulfilled by the **Teamworker** (TW).

■ Towards the later stages of projects, loose ends need tying up and quality control is needed, to be ensured by the presence of a **Completer Finisher** (CF).

Chapter 7

Unsuccessful teams

Our experimental work in building teams to various design specifications and then testing them out in competitive situations gave us the opportunity to look at teams which might otherwise never have come into being. To be allowed to compose a team of deliberately poor design is a rare privilege. No manager would ever set about or be allowed to set about such a task. The virtue of studying a badly composed team is that it furnishes valuable information about what can go wrong. Basic principles can be established and cause and effect examined. Knowing what to avoid can become one of the arts in good design.

Before we examine the characteristics of unsuccessful teams, a few words might be said about the problem of carrying out this particular investigation. Losing teams create more embarrassment for their members than winning teams; and the difficulties were greater in the executive management exercise (EME) than in Teamopoly.

The latter exercise offered the advantage of being under our own control and we were aided by the fact that the participants had come to learn about team-building and nothing more. The strain of failing could be endured provided it did not last too long.

Members of the newly formed companies would convene for a drink before lunch and 5 hours later, by the time dinner was due, the exercise was finished. Victors and vanquished toasted their success or drowned their sorrows accordingly. Later that evening they went off on their separate paths to conduct their inquests and prepare their presentations for the following day.

For the most part, the companies that finished last accepted their reverse in good humour. Whether failure reflected the design, usually deliberate in the construction of the team or a failure to use the resources of the team in the best way, there were lessons to be learnt. That, after all, was the reason they were attending the seminar.

The Henley EME was a different proposition. In the first place the game extended over a longer time span; at the beginning of our experiments it occupied one period every day, lasting in all one week. Secondly, team-building was not the reason for the management game, although it was embraced within it. The main purpose of the EME was to make managers more aware of 'the quantitative basis of decision-making'. The game occupied but a fraction of the 10-week course. The duration of the whole indicated the scale of investment that a firm or institution was making in the development of the manager chosen to go to Henley. Naturally the career expectations of Henley members were high, and so was the length of the course.

The management game furnished them with the first real opportunity to test their ambitions by pitting themselves against others in a competitive setting. In such circumstances losing was not a matter to be taken lightly. In Teamopoly we could concoct bad teams with devilish cunning and delight and with impunity. At Henley it was a different matter. We were under pressure not to construct wholly bad teams and it was considered politically desirable that every company should be given a reasonable chance of winning. Our poor designs had therefore to be watered down so that they became less extreme examples of the type. Yet in spite of their restrictions, basically the same patterns emerged in both our management exercises.

The characteristic features of unsuccessful teams were judged by scrutinizing the design of companies that tended to finish last, that usually fell into the bottom half of the results table and never won. This strict criterion meant that we had to remove Apollo teams from our well-defined group of ineffective teams. An occasional Apollo team did win. Their general results were poor but failure was not inevitable. By contrast some teams were so poorly constructed that they never overcame the disadvantage rendered by their composition.

Morale – an uncertain factor

After collecting our sample of consistently unsuccessful teams we set about examining the observer records of their performance in the EME or our own notes in the case of Teamopoly. We were able to draw up a league of demerit, having at its head the feature of team design most certain to ensure failure. But we discovered one interesting point. Unsuccessful teams do not necessarily suffer from poor morale or poor apparent teamwork. Poor morale may reveal itself – and it usually did – as a consequence of failure or of diminishing fortunes but it should not be seen as its cause. Some of the companies finishing with abysmal results started out as happy teams: even at the end members sometimes commented on how much they had enjoyed working with one another. 'They went down smiling' was a typical comment by onlookers.

Intense personal conflicts between members did arise in a number of companies but these conflicts did not necessarily presage poor results. In other words the relationship between morale and results at the bottom end of the scale seemed a tenuous one.

Mental ability – an important factor

Because of the sensitive nature of the subject it is easier to report on the characteristics of 'worst team design' in this book than it was at the time, when running seminars or management games. This was certainly the case with the leading predictor of poor team results, which was uniformly low scoring on the measures of mental ability. Even one good scorer could make all the difference to the outcome, especially if he was either a good Plant (PL) or a good Monitor Evaluator (ME). The lesson is that every management team needs to have within it one person, at least, who is clever, whether in an analytical or a creative sense. Unless there is someone effective in the sort of Team Role that a clever person carves out for himself, that company will be heading for trouble.

This generalization is applicable to virtually every situation in which a management group holds major responsibilities. The principle is seldom stated as boldly as it has been here, but empirically it seems to be followed in practice by the more successful industrial and commercial enterprises. The recruitment of graduates, however irrelevant their academic discipline, is the uncomplicated way in which firms ensure that they secure their requisite share of managers with good mental ability. Sophisticated companies go a good deal further than this, as we shall see in our next chapter. The assessment of mental ability has become a standard procedure in the search for potential managers, and our results indicate that this is rightly so.

The failure on the part of companies to obtain an adequate proportion of managers with good mental ability can scarcely be due to a conscious search for managers of low intelligence. That unintended result is simply a by-product of overvaluing a particular factor in recruitment that is found to have a negative association with mental ability.

Negative selection – a significant factor

Here it is useful to consider the concept of negative selection. This term refers to a recruitment process that, while being designed to achieve one intended effect, becomes more important for its unintended effect. The real effect is the filtering out of the very candidates of which the company stands in need. A typical example is where a company in a state of continuous decline looks for a general manager capable of causing its fortunes to recover but insists that the advertised salary is kept in line with the already depressed salaries of its current senior executives. This recruitment arrangement is ideally, though unintentionally, designed to exclude just the sort of general manager who would best fit the bill.

An instance of negative selection in the context of mental ability is well illustrated by the following case of a company that has earned itself a reputation for unsuccess.

CASE STUDY – A COMPANY NOT KEEN ON GRADUATES

Multigate is a large engineering group mainly centred on the Midlands. Although the company grew as a result of mergers to become the conglomerate that it is today, many of its characteristics echo the views and values of its now deceased but not forgotten founder.

Bert Rawlings was a self-taught engineer with drive and vision, who had started in business on his own account at a very early age. He was a practical man in both its positive and its more restrictive senses. On the one hand he had a genius for making things work while on the other he had a dislike, or even contempt, for anything he considered theoretical. This distinction was of no particular importance so long as he himself worked closely with those who held key executive positions in his company and he could assess personally the competence of his colleagues. The bond of shared experiences opened up the avenues of communication. But he was much more ill-at-ease when he had to confer with the men whose backgrounds differed from his own and who had to be judged by their arguments and advice rather than by what he saw as any real evidence of their practical competence.

As Bert Rawlings's company grew in size he endeavoured to surround himself with those who had come up the hard way and with whose thinking and attitudes he felt most at home. His choice fell largely upon apprentice-trained engineers. Through internal promotion they were appointed to the senior positions in the company while outsiders were rigorously excluded and graduate recruitment was non-existent.

Had Bert endeavoured to broaden his appointees through further education and training there might have been something to be said for this policy. But Bert's company was conspicuous by its abstention from all the various facilities and courses that were on offer for the development of managers. After Bert's death the company continued to grow on a rising market and in the search for economies of scale merging with other companies in the process. Nevertheless on the personnel front the old traditions remained. Bert Rawlings's men were the cast from which Multigate managers were drawn.

The first downturn in the market had a particularly severe effect on the fortunes of Multigate. The market recovered, then oscillated, but the company was now set on a downward path. In the face of impending financial collapse one new chief executive followed another. Eventually Multigate underwent a change of ownership and then started recruiting graduates, but the culture was unreceptive and no real change of character resulted until eventually that formidable outsider Spikey Smart was brought in on a rescue mission.

New managers usually bring about changes in the top management team. It had happened before in Multigate and in this regard Spikey Smart was following precedent. But this time there was a difference. The newcomer boldly required those executives he had inherited in responsible positions to be 'assessed' and as part of this process arranged that they should take intelligence tests. The move was not well received by those concerned. But Smart got his way. The distribution of scores amongst Multigate executives compared unfavourably with those of executive populations in other branches of industry. Here was further backing for those executive changes that Smart now felt impelled to make.

Whether Smart had consciously suspected it or not, the personnel policy begun by Bert Rawlings was an instance of negative selection based on intelligence. In other words a person of very high intelligence would have been unlikely to have ended up as one of Bert Rawlings's executives. The reason was straightforward enough.

In the founder's day, apprentice engineers were recruited overwhelmingly from those who left school at an early age. With few exceptions they were drawn from the streams of lower educational ability in the school. The system of sorting pupils into the type of school which the educational authorities considered suitable for their abilities depended upon an assessment at a critical age. Intelligence tests played a part in this examination. Hence those who performed poorly in these tests were more likely to get into the stream from which apprentice engineers – and the eventual Multigate executives – were recruited.

The Multigate example is a reminder of one of the strongest predictors, under experimental results, of factors associated with company failure. A general set of poor or indifferent scores on mental ability in the management team seems to preclude the chances of eventual success. If a single factor had to be singled out as posing the gravest risk, this might be the one to select.

Personality – a critical factor

Although mental ability usually has a fair spread amongst the executives of most firms, firms differ a good deal from one another in their cultural milieu. This is seldom due to any isolated cause. The explanation is more complex and has something to do with the culture of the firm. The variations in company culture give firms different personalities. Some firms are typically extrovert, being generally social and outward-looking; they thrive on new stimulus but are inclined to be casual when it comes to follow-through. Other firms seemingly have introvert personalities; they are self-sustaining and inclined to withdraw into themselves, pursuing internally generated goals with a certain relentlessness. Again the culture becomes a moulding force creating a type of collective personality. Individual executives whose private personalities contrast with the personality of the firm usually end up acting in accordance with the cultural norm which the firm engenders.

The concept of a firm's personality is worth considering in a general way. Anxious Introvert (AI) companies, in our early experiments, tended to perform poorly. Members of AI companies were often Specialists who had risen through their speciality into management. In spite of their advancement they were still prone to act like Specialists, failing to take a rounded view of the problems confronting them.

Some firms in the high-technology field appear to have a typical AI culture. The greater role and voice which Specialists have in them results in a pattern of activities that is reminiscent of the general behaviour of AI companies in the EME. A single-minded concentration on particular ends can give rise in practice to what M.F. Woods of the University of Bradford's Management Centre has called the Concorde Syndrome. Woods' letter to *The Guardian* in which he expands on this danger is worth quoting in full.

THE CONCORDE SYNDROME

One factor seems to have been omitted from the discussion on the Finniston report on engineering. I would term this factor the Concorde Syndrome.

British industry – in direct contrast to Germany and Japan – goes for the large spectacular project. In the public sector I can list Princess, Brabazon, TSR 2, Bevercotes (NCB Automated Pit), Magnox, AGR, etc.

The examples in the private sector are less publicized but no less damaging – the RB 211 is classic. We go for huge 'quantum leap' projects with high risk and ignore the personally boring, but commercially rewarding, business of doing what we already know better, planned progression into well-researched market driven areas. In fact, we may be accused of lack of professionalism.

The Concorde Syndrome is due to unbalance – of risk, but, most importantly, of management teams. An engineer or a marketing man or a chemist is allowed to run away with a project and the remainder of the skills are ignored.

To press the case for the engineer will not help the Concorde Syndrome or reduce its gross attrition of our material wealth. Getting the specialist into professional management teams is a different matter altogether.

Composition of unsuccessful teams

When it comes to considering what can be done about the problem, ineffective management teams can be classified as falling into two types. There are those which are products of the culture so that the faults of the management team epitomize the faults to which the firm as a whole has long been subject. In such cases changes in the management team may have only marginal effects. The second type of ineffective team has no deeply rooted causes but is linked with an unfortunate combination of characters. Remedial action may not be easy as socially contentious issues are involved, subtle factors are operating, and diagnosis is not obvious.

Typical instances of the latter type of ineffective team occur where obstacles prevent individuals finding their preferred Team Role. This can be true for any Team Role. It can be true too for individuals who are good examples of the Team Role type. The following companies illustrate poor design combinations associated with an otherwise useful person.

A Co-ordinator (CO) along with two dominant Shapers (SHs) both above average in mental ability. (The CO will almost certainly fail to get the job of Chairman.)

A PL in a company with another PL, more dominant but less creative, and no good candidate to take the chair. (The PL will be inhibited and will probably make no creative contribution at all.)

An ME with no PL and surrounded by Team Workers (TWs) and Company Workers of highly stable disposition and good mental ability. (The team is likely to generate a climate of solid orderly working and not foresee any need to evaluate alternative strategies or ideas.)

An Implementer (IMP) in a team of IMPs with no PL and no Resource Investigator (RI). (The company will lack direction and the organisers will not have much to organise.)

A Team Worker (TW) working with TWs, IMPs, and Completer Finishers (CFs) but no RI, PL, SH, or CO. (A happy, conscientious company will be over-anxious to reach agreement so that the presence of another TW merely adds to the euphoria.)

An SH working with another SH, highly dominant and of low mental ability; a Superplant, anxious and recessive; plus two or more IMPs. (The SH will find that any display of drive and energy on his part is likely to increase provocation and aggravation and disturb further an already unbalanced team).

An RI with other RIs and PLs but no TWs, CFs, MEs, or CO. (A formula for a talking shop in which no one listens, follows up any of the points, or makes any decisions about what to do.)

A CF with MEs and IMPs but no RI, PL, or SH. (The CF if he intervenes at all will probably only help an already slow-moving company to get bogged down in detail.)

All these cases exemplify someone who can potentially make a valuable contribution to a team but who is unlikely to do so. His natural Team Role will be blocked either by the apparent lack of need for it or by the presence of competing persons. That does not mean that his Team Role will be enacted by another. Where too many cooks spoil the broth it is probably the case that no one cook succeeds in doing much of the cooking. Equally the cooking can be obstructed by having other people around who only serve to get in the way.

The firm that in real life is faced with this problem need not be too pessimistic about its prospects. Some recombination of people may yet produce an effective team. A Managing Director of a large group once expressed the remedy with a neat turn of phrase: 'If things are not working out, you just shake the bag.' Even random rearrangements are capable of producing improved results.

Team members with no team role

Badly composed companies in our experimental teams usually featured Team Role clashes, overlaps or voids. In the case of Teamopoly we deliberately set about making these poor mixes. In that way managers became more aware of the nature of the problems poor team design could bring about. Whether a manager acquiesced in the problems confronting him or struggled to get more out of the team by adjusting his own Team Role, there were lessons to be learned.

We now come to a more personalized factor that often attaches itself to the ineffective team; this is the presence within it of a member or members who can be counted as liabilities rather than assets. This does not mean that the team design is basically at fault. It is simply that some individuals do not fit at all well into any team, detracting from a team's potential rather than adding materially to it. For about 30% of managers we tested, we could find no appropriate Team Role. These indefinite characters, who were not without ability, contained a higher incidence of problem people than we would expect to find in any cross-section of managers. Here are three typical examples.

THREE CASE STUDIES

Mr. Blank is a man whose test scores suggest high mental ability although he is clearly not creative. His cleverness, however, is not easily put to advantage because as part of his highly extrovert tendencies he reacts to everything in a highly spontaneous way. He talks first and thinks afterwards. This rules him out as an ME and he cannot make a PL. His self-control scores in the Personality Inventory are low and his constructs show a good deal of egocentricity. There is no prospect that he can make an IMP or a CO as he lacks the basic self-discipline. He is not social enough to be an RI or a TW and he lacks the urgency of a CF or an SH. Nevertheless because he is exuberant and mentally sharp he is likely to exert a major influence on how the team operates. The danger is that he will spoil a team's chances and unintentionally stop others emerging in their best Team Role.

Mr. Towers is a man of low mental ability but very high dominance and self-confidence. He is too cavalier in his approach to make an SH and his constructs on the PPQ are rather more orientated towards Justice than Achievement. Hence he is preoccupied with the rights and wrongs of the world rather than getting things done. He is full of hope while things go well. But once his team drifts into difficulties he is more interested in finding excuses than with putting things right.

Mr. Sittman has moderate mental ability and high anxiety scores. However, he has no interest in practical detail and has low scores on the Control Scales of the Personality Inventory so there is no prospect of his becoming a CF. He is too recessive and inward-looking to make an SH. As soon as the team meets its first reverse he is liable to become demoralized. The other team members do not know what to make of him. If he is given responsibility he may discharge it poorly, covering up any mistakes he has made. His self doubts are apt to become obstacles to action. He gives up easily but never formally contracts out of his responsibilities. This makes it difficult for others ever to take over anything he has been doing or to recognize what has gone wrong.

Managers who are liabilities in a team pose less serious problems than those who have a certain wrecking streak. These seem to be managers with a high capacity for spontaneous action, keen wits, and a disinclination to consult others. Fortunately they are few in number but they can go a long way in industry where conditions allow them the opportunity. At an early stage in my industrial career I encountered a remarkable personality in this mould.

CASE STUDY – A MANAGER WHO CAUSED DIFFICULTIES

Ed Rushton was the Sales Manager of a company in a high technology process industry. Unlike his predecessors, he took a keen interest in what went on in the laboratory. Whenever there was the merest hint that some experimental development could have some favourable implication for sales, he would wander round the laboratory unannounced and talk to people on his own. The extent of his interest was remarkable considering that he had not been with the company for long and had no technical background. One day he was shown the results of trials with a new material by a junior laboratory worker who was somewhat lacking in caution about its virtues and prospects. Rushton seized a specimen of the material and ran from the laboratory. Later the management learned that leading customers had been told about this new breakthrough and dates for eventual production had even been mentioned. This was embarrassing as the development was at an early stage. It was even doubtful that the trial material would become a production proposition at all. Undismayed by the faux pas, Rushton was soon forging ahead with another policy initiative of his own choosing when he was at last called to account. In the ensuing showdown Rushton departed with a golden handshake. After a short interval Rushton turned up again as the Managing Director of a major competitor. What happened in that company is uncertain but in due course 'after a policy disagreement at Board level' Rushton was removed, receiving a large amount for the termination of his services. Rushton was next heard of in an entirely different field as Chairman of a conglomerate industrial holding company. After only 2 years in that position the appointment ended, with Rushton receiving what at that time was believed to be a UK record sum as compensation for loss of office.

Managers who fail to fit into any management team tend to move from one appointment to another. In so doing they amass a track record which facilitates a rapid rise to the top; on the other hand, managers who fit well into a top management team tend to stay put. The Team Role qualities of a manager are seldom taken into account because management lacks relevant data to help them in the selection of managers or in the choosing of colleagues.

Unknown elements in teams

There were occasions in our experiments when we too lacked data about the managers who were being placed in teams. Over the years an average of between 10% and 15% of members failed to take the tests. Some of these were overseas members, a little bewildered on their arrival from Africa and Asia, who, seeing that the tests were voluntary, availed themselves of the respite from the general pressure of course demands. The U.K. drop outs included some who were busy preparing a speech or report and from time-to-time sporting enthusiasts who found the attraction of playing squash greater than that of taking tests. But the greater number of members who declined to take the tests did so from some positive objection. They did not believe in tests; they saw them as an invasion of personal privacy; they mistrusted the assurances that the information would be treated as confidential and suspected that the results would be leaked in some way to their employers.

Placing members who did not take the tests into teams became a highly speculative business. We could only guess as to what they might be like. We could not impute to them any particular Team Role. They were therefore excluded from team designs of any special interest. Instead they would land up in a rag-bag team of people who were left over from the other teams we had composed. On more than one occasion we made up teams entirely of people who had not taken the tests. But whatever arrangements were made for them they seemed to increase the accuracy of our predictions – non test-takers were strongly associated with companies that failed (usually finishing bottom). This was especially likely to be the result if they took up any key position of responsibility within the company.

We cannot be sure why individuals unwilling to volunteer for tests tended to perform less well than those who did volunteer. Was it part of a more general proneness to suspicion that was detrimental to teamwork? Or could it have been that a sense of embarrassment or even guilt in not taking the tests militated against a positive approach in the exercise? There was no objective reason why they should have felt exposed. None of their colleagues knew who had taken the tests and who had not unless they themselves volunteered the information. The only consequence of substance for the non test-takers was that they did not have an interview with me to discuss their best Team Role in groups. Here they were similarly placed to those whose test results did not suggest much of an affinity for any particular Team Role. These individuals for the most part also turned out to be indifferent team performers.

It looks as though those with no evident Team Role are at some disadvantage in comparison with those who can find one. A person with somewhat marked idiosyncrasies was often pleased to find that these had important Team Role implications. A quiet, rather dry man with good analytical ability but slow to make up his mind may in the past have regretted that he was not a dynamic manager; but now, he would be relieved to find he was a classic ME. New possibilities would be opened up for him and he would strive to develop those team talents that he found latent within him.

Indefinite team role teams

Some companies that we composed comprised people with classic Team Role profiles, while other companies were formed from people with indefinite Team Role profiles. The members of the latter seemed less concerned about the part they could best play in a team and tended instead to gravitate towards the job which technically they knew most about.

How this worked out may best be illustrated by a condensed account from an observer report in the EME.

CASE STUDY – NO CLEAR ROLES

Five of the members arrived promptly and began looking through their notes. After a few minutes JR suggested that the first task was to elect a Chairman. JP announced that he didn't want the job in any circumstances as he was already involved in two chairs. Similar noises were made by the others. When TF walked into the room JR said jokingly: 'You've got the job'. TF agreed that if it would help he was ready to be Chairman. The remaining board positions were filled by people volunteering for jobs most in line with their experience; RW, Finance; JR, Marketing; JP said he was prepared to take on Production and Purchasing and he also said that PB's experience should suit him for Management Services. WG's legal background equipped him to be secretary . . . Each member of the team worked on his own or with another.

There was little planning and co-ordination work within the group and the Chairman was very passive, until the time came when the forms had to be filled in. Policies were then discussed but each person ended up by taking responsibility for decisions in his own area . . . The group seemed to work co-operatively and to be enjoying the exercise . . . There was gloom when the bad results were announced.

Importance of corporate thought

If every manager carries out his functional responsibilities in a professional way, the company must do well – or so it is said. The facts often tell a different story, whether in a management game or within the normal operations of the firm. What fails to be taken into account is the way in which departmental objectives are capable of conflicting with one another. Any major change in one department can affect other departments. The ineffective company is the company where top managers remain locked within departmental patterns of thinking and cannot develop a corporate view.

CASE STUDY – DEPARTMENTAL THINKING

The distorting effect of departmental thinking at top level is well illustrated by a large company that supplied components widely used in the consumer durable market. In its early days when there were few good suppliers it was dominated by Production and run by an able autocrat in a highly authoritarian style. The company was able to supply the much-needed goods and it grew rapidly. Later it lost ground as other competitors came on the scene. The autocratic Chief Executive then moved to the holding group and sales. The company now concentrated on studying and meeting its customers' needs. Large stocks of finished goods were built up and the service offered to customers gradually allowed it to acquire a semi-monopolistic position and with it high profitability. A general recession combined with structural changes in the market then coincided with the retirement of the Chief Executive. He was succeeded by a man with less general experience but a keen interest in finance. As cash flow problems began to develop, massive cuts were made in the company's stocks and in the amount of money tied up in them. This produced in the short term startlingly good results. But later when the consumer durable industry, which had overreacted to the recession, found itself short of parts, the company was unable to respond in time. New competitors entered on to the scene to take advantage of the supply gap. The profitable semi-monopolistic position was lost and the once thriving company now found itself struggling to maintain its trading viability.

The Team Role approach to management allows corporate thinking to develop and protects firms from the hazards of functional dominance. There are real dilemmas in the objectives, policies, and priorities between which organisations have to choose. It is better that the issues are thrashed out in an effective but dispassionate way by the management team than that they are glossed over or that one particular manager should be allowed to dominate proceedings.

Acting against type

So far the pattern of ineffective management teams has been considered as a function of design fault. Enough was learnt about badly composed teams in the experimental work to enable us to predict with some confidence which teams were destined to become losers. Not all failures, however, could have been forecast from the outset. Some companies that seemed well equipped in all ways somehow managed to snatch defeat out of the jaws of victory.

These unpredictable failures were particularly associated with reversals in Team Role. What is meant by this is that a person who was a natural for one Team Role would take on another. Once such a change had been made the whole company was liable to get out of step. In one memorable instance we had placed a dynamic SH into a talented but rather weak company to give it thrust. The SH duly became the Chairman but then acted like the most passive type of TW. The company finished up in bottom place. The unexpected explanation for the SH's behaviour was that he had recently been taken to task by someone for his excessively forthright and aggressive behaviour. Thinking he must learn the lesson he had overcompensated. It was a pity, of course, that he had not learnt how to be a good example of an SH instead!

The more usual type of unexpected failure results from a poor allocation of manpower resources within the team. An ideal CO becomes the Secretary and an anxious TW is appointed Chairman. The PL does the data gathering and recording and a rather rigid IMP takes over negotiation. An RI with low critical thinking takes over planning while the CF becomes responsible for developing new strategies. Fortunately the mismatch is rarely as bad as that but even a small mismatch can rapidly bring about a reversal of fortunes.

Teams can use their internal resources to good or poor effect. The more conscious they are of where their strengths and weaknesses lie, the easier it is to adjust to that information. The lower this awareness, the greater the danger of making strategic mistakes that spring from self-delusion. As we have mentioned in previous chapters, that is in all probability why companies with members who declined to take the tests did so badly.

Summary

■ Unsuccessful teams were mainly characterized by an over-emphasis on a particular ability or Team Role.

■ Teams were not successful when individuals took on a role that was not suited to their personalities.

■ Teams were unsuccessful where key roles were required but never filled.

Chapter 8

Winning teams

The whole world is interested in winners. An Olympic gold medallist may beat the silver medallist in a race by 0.1 of a second but the great majority of people treat the two competitors as being in different classes. It was much the same in our experimental studies. Our long-standing focus on prediction as a means of testing the theory and technique of team design excited the recurring and restricted question: did you pick the winner?

Whereas many people supposed that our only object was to produce *the* winning team, in reality we were equally interested in getting right the approximate rank order of all the teams. As a task the former would have been much easier. Other teams could have been starved of the most useful people. Instead we had the more difficult task of making fine distinctions between teams. The team that we forecast as coming second had to be 'quite a good team' but not so good as the team forecast as coming first.

Prediction

Although our main concern was not to produce one winning team so much as to make a generally accurate forecast, there is something of value to be gained for the purpose of this chapter in focusing our attention on the companies that actually won. What were they like? And what have we to learn about their composition and operation?

Before we begin to answer these questions we must concede that it was more difficult to predict the team that would finish first than the one that would finish last. Experience soon taught us that a team can have such a membership that even before it convenes it has no hope of performing anything but badly. On the other hand, a team which on paper looks very good may disappoint in practice. One small unforeseen factor could spoil the otherwise promising pattern. A loss of interest for personal reasons by some key person might undermine the collective effort; the absence of one member could enforce some re-allocation of jobs that would not turn out well; or a company might fail to capitalize on a winning advantage through over-confidence after a runaway start. Admittedly a well-composed team has enough talent and resilience to recover from any reverse and to end up with a result that is at least respectable. But companies placed first in our forecast did not necessarily win – though they usually occupied one of the first three places and none ever finished last.

A composite picture of the typical company that figured most prominently at the top of the results table can now be built up. Of the various contributing factors, the most positive indicators were:

■ The attributes of the person in the Chair,

■ The existence of a good Plant (PL),

■ A spread in mental abilities,

■ A spread also in personal attributes laying the foundation for different Team Role capabilities,

■ A distribution in the responsibilities of members to match their different capabilities, and

■ Finally, an adjustment to the realization of imbalance.

These points, some of which have been alluded to earlier, now seem worth enlarging upon.

1. **The person in the chair**

   Here it proved important that there should be an affinity between the measured personal attributes of the person in the Chair and the good co-ordinator profiles that our research had identified (see Chapter 5). This formula portrayed the successful chairman as a patient but commanding figure who generated trust and who looked for and knew how to use ability. He would not dominate proceedings but he knew when to pull matters together if a critical decision had to be reached or a meeting had to close. In practice he always worked with, rather than against, the most talented contributors to the group.

2. **The existence of one strong PL in the group**

   Winning companies were characterized by the inclusion of a PL who was a good example of the type. Expressed in everyday language this meant that a successful company needed one very creative and clever member. Creativity could be treated as an entity in itself and distinct from high intelligence and analytical ability (which might be termed cleverness). In this sense, creativity in a PL was more important than cleverness, but if both were combined at a high level in a single person this was a great advantage.

   Creativity and cleverness, however, both had abrupt lower thresholds. For example a clever and very creative PL could be a great asset to a company whereas a very creative PL of only average cleverness was unlikely to make the grade, usually by failing to establish any Team Role credibility in a company. The failure of a PL to fulfil his or her potential in the team was the most distinguishing mark of apparently excellent companies that were in fact non-winners. PLs that disappointed were sometimes found to be creative in an inappropriate way; for example they were literate rather than numerate or had little interest in the undertaking.

3. **A fair spread in mental abilities**

   The spread in measured mental abilities appeared to have a material bearing on *company* fortunes. The best results were associated with *companies* containing one very clever PL, another clever member and a Co-ordinator (CO) who had slightly higher than average mental ability. This whilst other members of the company were slightly *below* average in mental ability.

   This formula is certainly not one at which we might have arrived by chance experience or by common sense. Yet with hindsight some of the advantages of this pattern are easily seen. A brilliantly clever and creative PL is an asset to a company, but only if ultimate responsibility lies with another.

A visionary also needs the stimulus of another lively mind of similar calibre on whom it is possible to sharpen his or her wits. Given that every group likewise needs someone able to find the flaw in imaginatively conceived but possibly unsound propositions, (the Monitor-Evaluator [ME] with his dry and intellectually dispassionate attributes). In the absence of an ME, another member of the group of the requisite mental ability could profitably interact with the PL. But it is not a good thing for this individual to be another PL. The two of them interacting will usually introduce specific Team Role competition.

The positive advantage of having other team members of slightly lower mental ability had puzzled us for a while. A possible explanation was that the gap between them and their fellow members caused them to look for other positive Team Roles: strong competition on one front had the effect of encouraging them to find ways of fulfilling themselves on other fronts. At any rate teams with a wide spread of scores in mental ability were observed to pull together better than teams that were intellectually more homogeneous.

4. **A spread in personal attributes offering wide Team Role coverage**
Winning teams were also characterized by a membership which offered a good spread in likely Team Roles.

In the executive management exercise (EME), winning teams seemed to need in particular one Completer Finisher (CF) and at least one Implementer (IMP). For our own Teamopoly exercise, which gave greater scope for negotiation, the Resource Investigator (RI) type of member figured prominently in winning teams.

In both exercises there were advantages in having one good example of an introvert and another of an extrovert. Although there were differences in pay-off behaviour between the EME and Teamopoly, if a general point is to be made it is that a winning company has a wider range of Team Role strengths on which to draw than less successful companies. Different types of ability increase the range of a team while also minimizing the unconstructive friction that occurs when two or more people compete for the same Team Role.

5. **A good match between the attributes of members and their responsibilities in the team**
One mark of winning teams was the way in which members found useful jobs and Team Roles that fitted their personal characteristics and abilities. It was impossible to forecast exactly how this would work out, but retrospective analysis of records suggested it as a feature of winning teams.

In general, it does not seem that people get the work they deserve. It is more common to find that individuals take on jobs most in line with their experience irrespective of how well they have performed. In the less successful teams, the allocation of work was dominated by the claim to have done something like it in the past.

Winning teams on the other hand found ways of reducing their reliance and dependence on one individual for a critical function unless that person had already shown signs of excelling. The way in which finance was sometimes handled illustrates the point.

Many companies placed responsibility for finance into the hands of a Finance Director, usually the person who claimed to have had most financial experience. In a number of winning companies, the risk of getting the wrong person in the job was minimized by a more flexible arrangement. For example, pairs of people would look after specific functions, one of which would be finance. A sharp-minded member could therefore work alongside someone used to dealing with figures.

The flexible pairing system also provided an opportunity for an able member to transfer attention to some other critical aspects of the company's activity, provided that person showed the inclination and had a useful take on the situation. In other words the best match between people and jobs came about through allowing informal arrangements. This modified any mismatches that would otherwise have existed.

6. **An adjustment to the realization of imbalance**
Weaknesses can be compensated for by self-awareness. While this is an accepted maxim governing individual behaviour, its truth can be extended to groups.

This sixth feature of winning teams came to the fore in Teamopoly. If it was less evident in our study of EME winners, the reasons are understandable.

During the early stage of the EME, the participants were either unaware of or had only a fleeting acquaintance with Team Role theory. It is rather doubtful whether partial knowledge did much to help their team effectiveness. In some instances it made inter-personal adjustment within a team more difficult. For example, some members who fancied themselves as PLs played their Team Roles in an overbearing and damaging way. They failed to take account of other Team Roles of which they had less appreciation and which could be critical at certain stages in company affairs. In fact, most of the real learning took place at the end of the exercise with the assistance of the debriefing: too late, of course, to influence personal behaviour.

In Teamopoly a very different situation prevailed. The seminar participants had already absorbed a fair amount of Team Role theory and technique, and had engaged in some practical reinforcement exercises before Teamopoly began. This experience did not, however, always result in adaptive behaviour. Once Teamopoly started, the excitement of the occasion caused many to forget what they had learnt. There was difficulty in appreciating how a general theory could be applied in practice.

However, there were some teams in which members consciously took account of their potential Team Role strengths, while being equally conscious of and compensating for their Team Role weaknesses. These teams, in making the most effective deployment of their resources, could become runaway winners, surprising themselves as much as others.

CASE STUDY – A COMPANY WHICH FACED THE FACTS

Our example came from the most recent team-building seminar we ran in Cambridge. The team was entirely composed of Shapers (SHs). To add to the disadvantage with which this unbalanced company was burdened, only one member had performed well in the measure of mental ability. In this respect the SH company compared unfavourably with the other three companies against which it was competing.

Once the team design had been published, the seminar participants were asked to make forecasts on the likely outcome of the exercise. The SH company was estimated as likely to finish last with the individual forecasts of the SH company members themselves according with the general verdict. When the SH company met for the first time its members took a doleful view of their collective prospects. In the event, however, the SH company not only won, but won handsomely.

What happened was explained frankly and unequivocally in the debriefing report by the SH spokesman. 'We realized that we had little chance of winning but we were determined to prove everyone wrong. Only one person had done well on the CTA. We concluded that as none of us had any brains we might as well make him the PL. 'Go away and think up some ideas,' we said. Then we remembered what we had been told about a good PL/CO alliance making for success. We reckoned that any one of us, being pretty managerial, could have acted as a good CO in the position of Chairman. We put it to our PL: 'You choose the Chairman you would like to work with.' From that moment things began to work well... But we couldn't stand having a PL around for too long. So we made him the board player. When he came back from board play he had added insights on which to work. While he was away we realized that we had to make the best use of our time. Being SHs, we knew we were likely to argue a lot. So we decided to take a vote on every issue. That enabled us to make quick decisions and seize opportunities. We progressively acquired an attractive portfolio of properties. From then on it was plain sailing.'

The value of seeing the important tasks in terms of the underlying Team Roles was well illustrated by several other teams unbalanced in composition but with a good deal of self-insight.

The prevailing pattern in self-aware teams was that at its first meeting the team would identify its area of weakness and then appoint someone to look after the jobs that looked as though they belonged naturally to the missing Team Role. For example, a team would discover that they lacked a CF. The implication was that deadlines and schedules would be forgotten. One member of the team would therefore be appointed to cover this aspect of the team's operation, usually the member regarded as having personal characteristics closest to the missing Team Role. The effect would be that the likely weakness of the team would not be exposed during the exercise, while the team would still succeed in playing to its strengths.

In other instances the discovery that a company had no PL led to a search for the nearest Team Role. This was usually that of the RI, who was likely to be the most enterprising, or the ME, who was likely to be clever. One of these two would then set about creating some new ideas and strategies appropriate to the challenge ahead. This often worked out pretty well. As the team would have other strengths, the overall performance of the company would be a good deal higher than might have been guessed at the outset.

To summarize about winning teams, their main feature was their strength in those personal qualities and abilities associated with the key Team Roles, together with a diversity of talent and personality making up the rest of the team. There was always someone suitable for any job that came up. Even teams with something less than the ideal distribution of talents could compensate for shortcomings by recognizing a latent weakness and deciding to do something about it.

Winning teams in industry

In due course it became plain that enough was known about winning management teams to transfer some of this experience to the industrial world. A company in industry, just like those of our simulation, could learn whether its management team had any obvious deficiencies. If deficiencies existed, it could take account of any shortcomings in recruiting to the management. Even without changing its composition it could do much to improve the way in which it used its own resources.

Two examples of this are particularly worth quoting.

Hilltown Engineering Ltd provides an example of how a single admission to a management team can change the fortunes of a company, initially in this case in a favourable direction. It also illustrates the rider: that a single subtraction from the team can have an equally momentous effect in the other direction unless the balance is re-established. Hence, some firms have winning teams only at certain periods of their life history. Others find a formula for maintaining their winning streak and do so through their culture. This is reinforced, and perhaps even promoted in the first place, by the way in which their personnel policies operate.

CASE STUDY – ONE APPOINTMENT MAKING ALL THE DIFFERENCE

Hilltown Engineering Ltd was the largest employer of labour in a rural town in the West Country. In spite of its good industrial relations and generally happy atmosphere, the firm's trading position had deteriorated until the holding company that owned it determined that something would have to be done. If no action were taken there was every likelihood that the firm would either have to be sold to a competitor or simply closed down.

Another possible line of action was to install another manager in a rescue bid and that was the line eventually chosen. Since the firm was closely tied to the motor industry and difficult times were foreseen, the manager designate needed to be a person of more than average drive and mental acumen, hard and tough yet at the same time someone who could retain the good industrial relations that had been built up over the years.

After many well-qualified candidates had presented themselves for the job, the eventual choice fell on John Bright, a manager in the CO/SH mould who had scored very highly in our measures of mental ability. As part of his apprenticeship John Bright attended our three-day team management seminar. The experience led to an in-company course, which while serving an educational role also helped to pinpoint some of the imbalances in the management team of Hilltown Engineering Ltd. This information was shared amongst the executives and also helped Bright to assess the new team which he was to inherit. As a result, a number of changes were made in general organisation and in the allocation of responsibilities and duties, although in person and number the management team remained much the same.

John Bright now set up a number of management project teams to examine all the various problems the firm faced. In the year in which he took over, the company was still making a profit but had been budgeted to lose £600,000 the following year. To add to this poor outlook a slump in the motor industry suddenly hit Hilltown Engineering Ltd. The company's best-selling product, manufactured under licence, was also threatened when the overseas company holding the licence announced that it was to be phased out.

To meet the gathering storm clouds, Hilltown Engineering Ltd moved fast. In Bright's second year the firm's complement was reduced from 1136 to 580 in an exercise that was remarkable for its smoothness; and the expected loss turned into a small profit. During this period a number of new ventures were started up. By the time of Bright's third year of office, the company had been hit by the international oil crisis and their best-selling product had been completely withdrawn. Nevertheless on a complement now reduced to 530 people, the company achieved a higher turnover than 3 years earlier when the work force had been more than twice as high. The net effect was a profit giving a 24% return on capital and in the following year, in spite of the unfavourable state of the market, a return of 21%.

The holding company now decided to promote Bright into a new job elsewhere. Unfortunately the effort that had gone into creating the team when Bright joined was not matched in recreating it after he left. Two years later the losses incurred were equivalent to an 11% loss on the capital employed and 1 year later this rose to a disastrous 43%.

Turning round a company that is failing is a more difficult operation than enabling an up-and-coming company to maintain its momentum and progress and avoid falling into those pitfalls which analysis of its management team composition might suggest as likely. An able management team can sense its own faults and do something about them. An example is Simpson Ltd, based in Adelaide, which became interested and involved in our team-building activities during my first Australian tour. By the time I returned 2 years later, I was surprised to find the good use to which the firm had put the knowledge it had gained. On this second visit all the senior executives took the tests. This enabled us to learn something further about the management team that ran Simpson and also provided a basis for seeing how the teams that we arranged for purposes of training performed in the Team-opoly exercise.

The seminars we conducted were much influenced by the concept of the classic mixed team and were about how that balance could be best adjusted either by

CASE STUDY – A SUCCESSFUL USE OF TEAM ROLES

The Simpson group operates in the home appliance white goods industry, being best known in Australia for its washing machines, clothes dryers and cookers. A progressive reduction of tariffs in Australia's hitherto highly protected market and too many producers operating in the home market had been amongst the problems which put the firm gradually into the red.

Eventually a new chief executive was appointed who set about the task of pulling the company round. The first step was to make a number of changes amongst the top executive appointments, which inevitably had an unsettling effect on the others. This disturbance was but temporary. Those executives whose services were to be retained in the key positions were assured that the company still wanted them. The vacancies that had been created were gradually filled with hand-picked young men of high ability. The

Continued

backlog of mistrust and suspicion was gradually overcome by an emphasis on open management.

Teamwork became the order of the day and served as the uniting force that linked older established members of the company with the new faces that had been promoted or introduced. Each product was now run by a multi-disciplinary management team. The experience not only had a maturing effect on the groups themselves but also on personal development. Individuals were spotted and judged as being suitable for joining other teams where their abilities could be better utilized.

After the various changes had been completed test results on the top management team showed a very good approximation of the classic mixed team pattern. The Team Roles of CO, PL, Team Worker (TW), RI, ME, and IMP were all well covered.

The effect of recruiting executives of high ability had, however, showed some signs of creating dangers of an Apollo syndrome elsewhere in the organisation. A high level of scores on mental ability was recorded, the highest of any company we had tested. Since some of the youngest managers recruited spent most of their time running their own sections, this had not so far created any obvious problems. But less impressive was the state of teamwork at this level.

In our Teamopoly exercise we decided therefore to set up a typical Apollo team. In spite of all the previous training in teamwork that Simpson had given, the Apollo team ran into the expected difficulties. Its members worked out and acted on their own approaches; conflicts were left unresolved and there was little co-ordination. The Apollo team finished poorly, a result which the other Simpson teams received with some amusement and a certain lack of sympathy.

Simpson's approach to management enabled the firm to make continuous progress so that it became one of Australia's most flourishing manufacturing companies. Over a period of 5 years, until the publication of the original *Management Teams*, the group volume of turnover increased four times in markets which themselves had shown little growth in total. Market share of the individual product businesses moved progressively from an average of 20–30% to an average of 55–85%. Profitability had increased by an average of 25% each year and the company's share prices quadrupled. The company was rapidly increasing its rate of investment and new overseas operations had been or were in the process of being set up.

recruitment of a suitable person to fill a gap or by Team Role adjustment within the team. This approach was governed by the fact that the classic mixed team had proved the most reliable of winning teams in our studies. A further consideration was that the concept was unfamiliar so that firms felt that there was something new to be learned. In fact it was very difficult to point to a firm that was already actively employing this concept.

Other successful patterns

The classic mixed team was not, however, the only type of winning team. Other patterns figured amongst the winners, less complex in character and more commonly encountered in industry than the classic mixed team.

The best runner-up in the results league was the team of co-operative stable extroverts. This type of team only occasionally won, but it frequently came second and seldom did badly. Its members did not contain any great spread of team types, being mainly TWs and RIs with IMPs as a secondary Team Role. Provided the team was well equipped with a reasonably good level of mental ability, they did not seem to suffer from lack of an ME or PL.

In fact the clear distinctions in Team Role in this type of company were less evident than usual. What they had missed in specialized behaviour they made up for in flexibility. 'All the world's a stage and one man in his time plays many parts'; and it was difficult at times to know who was playing which part. All the actors were heavily engaged. They loved working in teams, enjoyed each other's company, talked a great deal and discussed everything together. But the pattern was not as chaotic as it might seem to the casual onlooker. Animated interaction led to collectively produced ideas which seemed beyond their individual reach.

If there was one weakness to which this team was subject, it was complacency and euphoria to which stable extroverts tend in general to be prone. Eventually we were able to improve the design by introducing another extrovert of a somewhat different type, an SH. One SH adequately served a team of easy-going extroverts, ensuring that there was someone around to crack the whip whenever a discrepancy opened up between objective reality and a team's optimistic estimates of its own position.

Moving down the results league, two other types of winning team were found. Yet neither could commend themselves as patterns which others might follow. The reservation about both these team types is that their failures were no less conspicuous than their successes.

The first of these occasionally very successful teams was one in which the leadership was firmly in the hands of a superstar. More concretely, this was a team in which the Chairman would have unrivalled superiority in intellectual or creative ability over other colleagues. The position and the individual's natural talents reinforced each other in establishing ascendency. This allowed the company to operate a coherent strategy, to use flair to advantage and to make a quick decision when the occasion demanded. Morale amongst the team members would even stand up well provided the company was achieving results. Lack of opposition to the superstar Chairman made for streamlined operation.

With the right formula such a company could achieve good results but if there was anything wrong it would be slow to take corrective action. The dominant leader could provide an overall grasp that would enable a team to move forward unwaveringly to its objective but equally that leader might lead the flock up some blind alley, and none would think of turning back until the point of crisis had already been reached. Superstar-led teams had a way of hastening either to the top of the results table or to the bottom.

The final winning team that merits attention is the Apollo company. This has been fully discussed in Chapter 2. The Apollo company is one which hoards mental ability so that it has ample resources and talents for dealing with the most complex problems but suffers from extreme difficulty in being able to use what it has. In general Apollo companies performed poorly, but they did occasionally win. Under the right Chairman and with the right culture, sufficiently good, or adequate, teamwork could be established to enable their assets to be realized.

To take stock, several types of teams have figured amongst the winners. The first is the classic mixed team, where Team Roles tend to be well differentiated – by track record the most successful of all teams. The second is what might be called the typical participative group, comprising stable extroverts with a liking for group work and whose Team Roles tend to be undifferentiated. And the final two types are teams which either are led by or consist mainly of talented and clever people.

How far do these teams have emerged as the most consistently effective over the years in our experimental studies compared with the teams that run the most successful companies in the business world? Do the same underlying principles and patterns apply, or do they not?

Answers to these questions are not easy to provide. Certainly successful companies can be identified by their record of performance; the main difficulty lies in finding an adequate means of describing how these companies are run and who runs them.

Nevertheless some useful insights can be gained by looking closely at a few very successful companies which have features relevant to the theme of our inquiry.

Team practice in three companies

The United Kingdom has had a less than distinguished post-war industrial record. If we omit multinationals and confine ourselves to indigenous companies that have been consistently successful, we end up with a small field. From this group I have picked three, one each to represent distribution, industry and services.

Marks & Spencer, ICI, and the BBC. Marks & Spencer must be one of Britain's most successful retail stores, famed for its quality of product, its standard of service, the treatment of its staff, and its record of profitability. ICI has been chosen as one of Britain's biggest and most successful industries, a model employer, where high-level expanding technology and commercial success go hand in hand. The BBC commends itself on different grounds. It is a public corporation and not therefore subject to the normal commercial criteria. Its strength lies in its reputation. It has been hailed as Britain's best ambassador, and its most successful TV productions have made their mark around the world. One particular reason for choosing the BBC is that the success or failure of its TV production teams can, in a sense, be measured. Some programmes are so unsuccessful that they never see the light of day. Others attract a large viewing public and create their own export market.

Common features

Before we consider these companies separately we may note what they have in common. All three companies are heavy recruiters of University graduates. ICI annually recruits more qualified scientists than any other firm in the UK. The BBC recruits graduates not only for critical jobs, such as script writers, but also for a wide range of jobs that are intellectually undemanding. In the case of Marks & Spencer, about half of all assistant store managers are graduates, a figure unparalleled in the UK retail trade. Since all three organisations fill their senior positions almost entirely through internal promotion, it is clear that their personnel policy offers as candidates for the management team a steady supply of well-educated young men and women of good mental ability with in-depth experience of the industry.

CASE STUDY – A SUCCESSFUL RETAILER

Marks & Spencer has centrally located shops in almost every town of any size in the UK but, apart from a computer installation, the whole Marks & Spencer organisation is in fact housed in its Head Office in Baker Street, London. Such centralization could make the company very susceptible to rigidity, especially as it has a well-defined

---

Continued

management structure. This danger is offset by the importance given to the operation of its management teams and its communication groups.

The Board of Marks & Spencer consists of 22 directors. In practice most top management decision-making stems from the regular meetings of the chairman's Advisory Committee. This management executive group consists of the chairman and four regular members plus the occasional specialist who will be invited in as a resource from time to time. Every month the chairman will hold information meetings which up to 80 senior people will attend. Departmental managers will hold their own information meetings for between 10 and 20 people. At the level of the store, communication groups regularly meet. They usually comprise 12 or 13 people with each area of the store represented. Employees can raise any points they wish at these meetings, while at the same time they are told about all that is going on.

On the operational side, teams meet regularly at the Marks & Spencer Head Office to discuss any major plans and changes that relate to their area of the business. These meetings are easy to arrange since all the key people connected with any given section of the business are likely to be found on one floor of each block of offices that surround a courtyard. A feature of these business meetings is that, while the meeting is kept fairly small, several levels of the hierarchy are usually represented. The rather larger Merchandising Review, made up of 20 people, might contain members from 7 levels - the Director of the merchandising group, a senior executive, an executive, a merchandising manager, the merchandiser, a selector and a technologist. At these meetings the senior people are there as of right but those at junior levels have to be nominated by those above them. In this way some form of control is exercised over the composition of the meeting and juniors get an early chance to shine.

In addition to these regular meetings, informal meetings are frequent as part of a general policy of close co-ordination and as a means of ensuring that important points of detail receive close attention and are looked at from all possible angles. By the time a new member joins the top management team he will often already have become highly experienced as a team man. The social basis of management softens the effect of centralization thereby reducing the risk that the demise or retirement of any one key manager would produce an upheaval liable to undermine the viability and prosperity of any one business section or of the company as a whole.

Marks & Spencer and ICI are both examples of *winning* companies in their own separate fields. Both companies are highly participative and consultative in their social, business, and industrial relationships. But while Marks & Spencer is highly centralized, ICI places an emphasis on decentralization except on certain overriding issues.

CASE STUDY – A SUCCESSFUL INDUSTRIAL COMPANY

ICI is organised into 10 major divisions and also runs 9 subsidiary companies. Each division prides itself on its distinctive culture and values its autonomy. The way in which centralization and decentralization work together is well illustrated in relation to graduate recruitment. Like other large companies, ICI operates on the 'milk round' of British Universities. The initial exercise is undertaken by CURV (the Co-ordinated University Recruitment Venture).

The 'milkroundsmen' drawn from different divisions give initial interviews at the various universities to about half of those who complete application forms. A list goes to ICI Head Office which then circulates the divisions on short-listed candidates. That is where CURV ends. The divisions then adopt their own preferred selection procedures. Some divisions employ a comprehensive battery of selection tests to aid them in the selection process. Other divisions do not use tests at all. Divisions that use tests do not necessarily employ the same test battery. Within a division there may even be differences of practice: for example, mechanical engineers will be carefully screened with the aid of selection tests, while chemical engineers are not, the difference being accounted for merely by the differing viewpoints of the managers in these sections. However there are common rules that apply: all appointees are offered specific jobs within the section of those who interview them and divisions are not allowed to 'top' an offer when they are competing for the same candidate.

In spite of certain differences in recruitment practice there are two factors which, taken together, have given a certain distinctiveness to ICI as a company over the years. The first factor is that great emphasis is placed on the academic calibre of those recruited. Only graduates with good degrees are considered, while there is also a tendency, rare in industry, to recruit those with research doctorates. There was even a time when PhD chemists were recruited to run chemical plants in the belief that this was the best way of getting hold of a high-calibre managerial elite. In due course other methods were found to yield more satisfactory results. Over the years methods may have changed but the aim of recruiting the 'best' has remained constant. The second common factor of note is the emphasis placed on group training once graduates are recruited. The clever young graduate is socialized almost as soon as he enters the company, not only by industrial training methods but by immersion in the culture of ICI. One academic study by a sociologist likened the company to a club. The club atmosphere acts as a powerful counter to the recruitment tendency that would otherwise turn ICI into an Apollo company.

The third UK *winning* company differs from our first two by being generaly much less concerned with participation, consultation, and group working. The BBC as an employer is referred to by many of its employees, as well as by outsiders, as Auntie. A certain avuncular patronage (or its feminine equivalent!) is part of its heritage. Yet arts graduates, as well as engineering apprentices, are strongly attracted to employment in the BBC. This gives the BBC the opportunity to take its pick of talented applicants, but creates a problem later on as to how they can best be absorbed into effective working groups.

CASE STUDY – A SUCCESSFUL SERVICE COMPANY

All television programmes are created by relatively small teams. In practice, teams are continuously forming and reforming. Every programme is a one-off event. Such a background makes it difficult to formulate a coherent and consistent personnel policy. People join programmes as they become available and by invitation.

The team formation process operates in a mysterious way: line management has a hand in it; a crucial influence is also exercised by those who have a major part to play in the programme. Key people feel the need for a greater say. Film directors, authors, script-writers, star actors, cameramen and cutting editors may all acquire reputations as distinguished professionals. Creative artists aspire to run programmes that give full scope to their own creative individuality; yet they all want to work with those who are at the top of their own professional tree. These two aspirations are not easily combined.

What is recognized by those with responsibilities in the area is that the BBC is in effect laden with PLs. PLs are often unreasonable about whom they are prepared to work with and the terms under which they are prepared to operate. But they are also capable of behaving in uncharacteristic ways. What is observed is that one PL may be such a star that other lesser PLs will be prepared to work with him or her by giving way on more points than usual in the cause of professional fulfilment.

Since this whole process involves a most complex pattern of human relationships and is somewhat unpredictable, management does not always intervene directly by insisting that particular individuals join particular teams. Recognizing that people can work with some crew members but not with others, management offers some latitude to the most talented performers, allowing them scope for creating their own teams. Other teams come together by mutual arrangement.

This policy has to be reconciled with a basic strategy of using available resources as fully and economically as possible. A certain amount of positive allocation of people is therefore necessary. There are a number of SHs/PLs who seem capable of putting into operation their own programmes but otherwise management has to engage in a delicate balancing operation in forming its production teams. By so doing, it assures the production of a limited number of television programmes of outstanding merit while also allowing the general output target of programmes to be maintained.

Team role theory and winning companies

If we relate these three enterprises to the conclusions we reached about winning teams under experimental conditions, we may see that each has found its own mainstream solution to the management team problem. In effect Marks & Spencer has developed a pattern that is in line with stable extrovert teams and this is broadly confirmed by what they appear to look for in selecting candidates. PLs are not needed in these teams, but a good general level of mental ability is assured by the nature of the recruitment process. Team members *prove* themselves in junior teams, and as they move between one team and another they generate material evidence in terms of which their suitability for promotion can be judged. Once Marks & Spencer had become a thriving company with sound policies that had stood the test of time, the problem of how to get a good management team largely resolved itself by a tradition that had been built up. Here it is fair to talk about the establishment of a Marks & Spencer culture.

In cultural terms there are in fact affinities between Marks & Spencer and ICI: the emphasis on care of the employee; the importance given to high standards; and belief in participation, consultation, and team working. But ICI requires its own distinctive 'solution' to the problem of recruiting the management teams which run its divisions. On the one hand it has the image of an establishment company – a headmaster once likened it to the Bank of England – but on the other, the prosperity of the company depends on continuous progress in pushing back the frontiers of science in a chemical and industrial setting against an international, rather than just a domestic, background. ICI therefore requires its share of clever pioneering people if its rate of progress is to be maintained.

The academic standards laid down for ICI entrants and its rigorous selection procedures ensure that it has an abundance of talent even at the risk of an overkill. The dilemma here is that the company is caught between serving its cultural and business aims. This danger is offset to some extent by the emphasis given to training the able graduates the company recruits in group work. The effect, then, is that the company is recruiting potential Apollo members whose individual talents are needed for the difficult tasks ahead, but is striving to ensure that it does not end up with typical Apollo groups.

The BBC, for its part, may be compared with ICI for the high standard it demands of its intake, though more specifically it seeks PLs. Like ICI, it risks an overkill to guarantee that it acquires the talent it demands. Apollo teams occur frequently and are recognized for what they are. They are often chaotic in style and atmosphere. But the experiences generated at least allow for the emergence, through survival of the fittest, of the superstar-led team. This is one of our four types of winning company – not a reliable one, but one which is capable at times of reaching the heights of achievement.

If there are any general features that govern successful companies in the business world, one may be that they have learnt to devise ways of operating like co-operative Stable Extrovert teams without actually recruiting Stable Extroverts. Winning companies are keen to ensure that they recruit candidates with high initial ability: they rely to some extent on the culture to ensure that those selected end up as proficient in team working.

The most successful team in our experimental studies – the classic mixed team – does not seem as yet to figure amongst winning teams in the business world. Why is this? It may be that such teams do exist but are very difficult to detect. Even so we might have expected to see more traces of them. Their scarcity, if real, may be explained on several counts.

First, the concept is not easily grasped, especially if the underlying complexities are to be understood; second, there is a natural human resistance to searching for the mixed team as a deliberate act of policy, for like selects like and people usually create groups in their own image; third, good material for mixed teams may be suspect in the eyes of company selectors who are often searching for the ideal rounded man. But as Shakespeare reminds us in *Measure for Measure:*

> *They say best men are moulded out of faults and, for the most, become much more the better for being a little bad.*

In the mixed teams there is always someone present to underpin a weakness and who will be fulfilled by so doing. Such a brief calls not only for good team working but also for both modesty and sophistication.

The implications of winning companies

What then are the implications of this chapter? In practice the classic mixed team provides the most consistently good results. But to put such a team together must be an intricate operation demanding high skills from the selector. Any disturbance of the team can easily upset the balance. This is why there is much to be said for forming a group whose members are less specialized in their functions and abilities.

Team-orientated stable extroverts, well disciplined and of reasonably good mental ability, produce consistently good teams, covering between themselves all the various functions that have to be performed. Such teams have the advantage that their members can be combined and recombined in other teams without much loss of efficiency. The firm that is committed to a consultative, participative style of management and seeks versatile, general utility managers can look for candidates who are typical members of our second type of winning team.

For very large companies this policy has much to commend it. The alternative option of moving towards the classic model of winning teams could be a formidable task. Large organisations are likely to experience difficulty in exercising control over the composition of their senior management teams since so many forces impinge upon the politics of promotion. Here small companies are at an advantage.

Our two other types of winning team are both capable of achieving great things though liable to founder.

The superstar-led team, where one highly talented or creative individual dominates his colleagues and leads 'from the front', has limited scope in large enterprises under prevailing social and economic conditions. It has to be remembered, however, that this pattern has met with considerable success in the past. If authoritarianism is to survive as a competitive system, this is a formula to give it life. In small firms the superstar-led team may still produce good results for a long time to come. Nonetheless it cannot be confidently recommended in any general way. Over-dependence on a single individual is a prescription for everlasting uncertainty over what the future offers.

The problem of over-dependence on a single individual is overcome when we look at the Apollo team, the type of team that we may expect to find running high-technology firms. Here the need to recruit well-qualified and able young men who can operate on the frontiers of technology predetermines the type of management that will emerge under these conditions. There are prospects that a few of these Apollo-run firms will prosper. A good Apollo Chairman or a rapid turnover of young Apollo managers allowing only the fittest to survive will increase the chances of success.

Winning companies vary in the character of the teams that manage them: yet after years of experiments in composing teams and encouraging others to try out their own designs and after much searching after successful examples in the industrial world, we must conclude that the choice in proven patterns remains strictly limited.

Summary

- Winning companies possessed good Team Role balance.
- Compensating for lack of balance can have a favourable effect on a team's prospects.
- Awareness of Team Roles helps to improve companies' performance.

Chapter 9

Ideal team size

How many people should we have in a team? To some extent the answer must depend on the amount of work that needs to be performed. But the notion of an ideal number is worth pursuing where members of a management team spend their time deliberating together. Before we look at the leads which our experiments can offer, a few points of a general nature are worth making about the effect of group size on behaviour.

Groups and individual behaviour

In general it seems that the bigger the group, the greater the unseen pressures that make for conformity. These pressures may become so prevalent in mass meetings, congregations, and assemblies that an appearance – or illusion – of unanimity is created.

Behaviour within the group is further complicated by group structure. The stronger the structure, the less tolerance there is for dissenters or for any form of deviant expression. Where groups are unstructured – that is to say large numbers of people meet for a purpose but without any imposed constraints – the individual, rather than recovering a sense of mature individuality, is apt to revel in the anonymity which size offers. A crowd freed from social control becomes a mob. One way or another, large gatherings of people exercise such an influence over their constituents that each person becomes either excessively passive, or, if full self-expression is permitted, inclined to irresponsible behaviour, aggressive verbal declarations, or even acts of destruction.

Why should the individual lose a sense of mature identity and ability to contribute in a positive way in large groups? Part of the answer may be that sheer numbers force each individual to play a non-role so that for the time being, at least, actual personality is diminished. It comes down to practicality. Consider, say, a meeting of a hundred people conducted along democratic lines with all members invited to contribute from the floor. Let us imagine that the Chairman wished every person to contribute equally and allotted time accordingly. Then for an hour each person would talk for 1% and listen for 99% of the time. With perfect regulation each speaker would have 36 seconds. This would make it impossible for anyone to say anything useful.

Teams of ten members

Now suppose we reduce the number in the meeting by a factor of 10. Suppose again that conversation is shared equally, with people talking in turn rather than simultaneously. Then each person will be talking 10% of the time and listening 90%.

While this arrangement sounds far more workable, it still means that everyone will be cast in a mainly passive role. What makes the arrangement less feasible still is that, in a peer group, individuals vary appreciably in their talkativeness. A dominant person will be disinclined to restrain himself for 90% of the time, while a recessive individual whose fair ration, as it were, is 10% of the talking time is more likely to say nothing at all. If a group contains several dominant people, the competition for talking space can lead to continuous interruptions or simultaneous monologues. This outcome seldom satisfies anyone.

While a unit size of 10 looks too large for a group of peers conferring in a team, it is a different matter once a group becomes formalized. The strength of a structure, one is aware, depends on the nature of the cells which make it up and on their arrangement. Here there are lessons to be learnt from the past. History must grant the Roman army the honour of being the longest surviving organisation based on power that the world has ever known. That army was arranged in multiple tiers with the person in charge at each level having 10 people reporting directly to him. A commander who addresses 10 people can do so without raising his voice and he can count on his fingers to ensure that they are all present. He can talk for most of the time, issuing instructions and directions, and there should still be time available for anyone to raise any queries or relevant observations. For a streamlined chain of command 10 looks the ideal number as the base unit for organisation. Perhaps it is no coincidence that the army of the Incas, the most enduring ancient civilization of the Americas, had a similar unit size and arrangement.

Aside from the work done by us with the Henley Management College, there was also work done by the college independently using syndicates. These syndicates consisted of 10 or 11 members – with a measure of authority being invested in an appointee – in this case a Chairman. Management education may not have been around as long as the Roman army but at least it can be said that this size of syndicate has proved itself since the College syndicate working began. The Chairman in controlling proceedings would draw on the resources of the group to enable a wide variety of views to be brought to bear on the subject or problem under review. By creating a need for listening, the essentially educational nature of the activity reduced the level of active participation to the point where 10 or 11 became a most suitable number. This group size offered advantages too for those periodic recreations which served to cement the personal bonds between syndicate members. Ten could fit into two cars.

Ten or 11 seemed to be a number that was large enough to give adequate variety in the possible range of social permutations that can enrich life but small enough to allow the syndicate to retain a sense of intimate group identity. It seems no coincidence that outside the village pub, to which the syndicate members were wont to retire, we find the village green on which eleven villagers play cricket during the summer; and in the field behind the pub we find the football pitch on which another team represents the village during the winter – again with eleven members. Can 10 or 11 be the ideal size of structured human groups involving close personal relationships?

If so, some might see in this an echo of the primeval male hunting band designed to use its strength and wits to advantage in the pursuit of large game. The quarry may have changed but the game remains, the meaning of the word changing to reflect a sporting match. The essentials of the team are retained too. The main difference is one of outward form as the carnivores sublimate themselves in team sport.

Medium-sized teams

The advantage of a unit of 10 or 11 members seems to recede when a team of this size meets around a table to thrash out plans and policies with a view to making decisions. There is scarcely enough scope for everyone to engage in a fair share of talking without unduly prolonging the decision-making business or reducing its efficiency. To disengage would also cause problems. It would be impolite to read a newspaper. Everyone has to look interested and attend. Nor does the purpose of the occasion provide the educational stimulus that the typical Henley syndicate enjoys and which, in a sense, occupies the unoccupied.

In an empirical way, and without any intervention on the part of the experimenters, Henley had come to the conclusion at an early stage that a company of 10 or 11 members was too large. A reduction was made to eight members. In time even this proved on the big side. In practice, an executive management exercise (EME) company tended to be dominated by two, three, or four prime movers. There would be one or two others marginally occupied and the remainder contributed little and became bored and dissatisfied.

The College then reduced the number to six. The six-man company was found to be a more stable and enduring group and the greater part of our experiments were therefore conducted in teams of this size. That then raised the more general question of whether there is an optimum size for a team meeting around a table.

At this point an obvious objection suggests itself. As we have previously identified nine complementary Team Roles and found the characteristics of individuals who best fit them, is there not a case for forming an ideal team of nine members? And, if so, why in the event should a team of six have proved more satisfactory?

The team of eight holds out promise but arouses misgivings. Its size is intermediate between, on the one hand, the ideal command group, and on the other hand, a small intimate circle who can act and talk together in concert at a mutually acceptable level of contribution and involvement without needing to interrupt each other.

Now it could be argued that a team of eight can reach its potential only if it is highly structured with a suitable person as Chairman and with its members appropriately selected and briefed so that the eight Team Roles are covered by a person well fitted to perform each one. That is a tall order. Even if eight people of the right type were assembled, it might still be difficult to ensure that they developed those mutual expectations that would allow them to interrelate in the theoretically ideal way. In any case such an intricate arrangement is hardly necessary. We have already observed that most competent managers seem able to function well in both a primary and a secondary Team Roles. In some cases, they are adept in three. In other words, we do not *need* eight managers to perform eight Team Roles. By a doubling up of Team Roles, four managers could cover all eight. On this model, the minimum number needed to cover all Team Roles would be five. That allows nothing for the overlap that is likely to occur between members in either their primary or secondary Team Role, nor does it necessarily allow any one person such as the Co-ordinator or the Plant to concentrate on a single Team Role.

Smaller teams

The number six therefore is a fair compromise figure, coming as it does between eight which, except as an ideal, is too big and four which, except as another type of ideal, is too small. Yet in practice a target *company* size of six was not always obtainable. Members of course do not always divide exactly by that number and it was not uncommon to have one or two *companies* of seven members. The seven-man *company* in terms of resources had a numerical advantage over the others. But this did not seem to be much of an asset. For some reason the seven-man *companies* did not perform so well as the six-man *companies*. It may be the former were just that bit too big to be efficient.

In the Henley management game (EME) the six-man *companies* portioned out their responsibilities along conventional lines. One person would be Chairman, a second would look after finance; a third, marketing; a fourth, production; a fifth, management services; and a sixth might combine purchasing with the job of acting as the Company Secretary.

This functional division of work allowed each member to establish his own work territory and avoided the conflict that overlapping responsibilities tend to engender. As most *companies* gave to their members those jobs which corresponded most closely with the work they normally performed, confidence was instilled through doing something that was familiar. Yet as the specific tasks that fell to each member of the *company* used up only a small proportion of their available time, the members had ample opportunity to play their parts in group discussion. It was this opportunity, derived from a degree of under-employment, that set the scene in which Team Roles were to emerge. A team of six could offer a broad range of technical skills and Team Roles so that a *company* could achieve, if its composition was favourable, a high degree of balance. This was valuable in itself as an educational experience. In general terms, it is not without significance that, for a period of at least a decade, six endured as the number that was found, on the internal evidence at Henley, to be most suitable for enabling a management team to tackle a complex problem.

When teams are involved in high rates of activity there is a danger that even a medium-sized team becomes inefficient since problems arise in coordinating its various parts. This was borne out in the case of Teamopoly – an exercise that made simultaneous demands on decision-making and action, and so created crises for a company in sorting out its priorities and dealing with conflicting urgencies.

Greater pressure was exerted by giving each *company* four members instead of six as in the EME at Henley. In many instances, the four members were brought together precisely because they were not complementary. All this was part of our design strategy to bring to the fore the differences in the behaviour of teams composed along different lines and to relate their behaviour to their Team Role composition. The four-man *company*, of whatever composition, could not cover all the vicissitudes and predicaments that came its way. Lack of time, though a source of difficulty, was not the prime problem. There were in fact periodic intervals during the exercise in which major strategic questions could have been sorted out. What is of interest is that every winning *company* in Teamopoly, including those of more orthodox design, made at least one major strategic mistake during the exercise. In the EME at Henley, on the other hand, there was less to criticize in the way that winning teams performed.

Under favourable circumstances, team balance was easier to achieve in the six-man *companies* of the EME than in the four-man *companies* of Teamopoly. If, in human resources, the four-man team tended to be less well equipped than a six-man team to tackle a complex problem, there were at least counterbalancing advantages. The four-man *company* achieved a level of intimacy, involvement, and excitement that the six-man *company* could never quite match. This does not mean that the team was more integrated; rather that relations were more intense. Love, hate, humour, exuberance, and exasperation abounded. One seminar member declared himself unable to say goodbye to a fellow team member for fear that tears would well up in his eyes. Yet another felt bound to register a complaint about a fellow team member. The four-man team engendered relationships not dissimilar to those that belong to a family where only a narrow margin separates the varied emotions that closeness brings. Just as all families are happy in the same way but unhappy families are unhappy in their own peculiar way; so also we might say of the four-man team: if they got on well they were harmonious and positive on all fronts; but where relationships did not work out, the cross-currents seemed immensely complicated.

The chairman and team size

One possible reason for the observed differences between teams of four and six revolves round chairmanship. With six in a team there was always someone in the chair. There was a certain cool formality about proceedings. On the other hand a team of four, though occasionally a chairman might be elected, more often turned into a leaderless group. It became unstable at moments of crisis. It operated well only when complementary Team Role relationships were established and depended on good Team Role design from the outset.

If a chairman is seen as one who holds the balance in a group, then number plays a part in his emergence. In a team of four, a chairman in the case of conflict has two on one side and one on the other. No casting vote is required. The job seems hardly necessary. In a team of six the emerging chairman would deal with two on the one hand and three on the other. Still no casting vote is called for; nevertheless, the greater team size suggests the need for someone to organise the resources of the group. Now take the intermediary team size of five. The case for a chairman here is overwhelming. The group is large enough to benefit from organisation, while the casting vote becomes decisive should uncertainty or disagreement threaten.

Five-man teams only occurred in our experiments in an unpremeditated way. With a target team size of six the number was occasionally and unavoidably reduced to five either because there were insufficient course members to make every *company* up to six or because of the enforced absence of a member of a six-man *company* from illness or other causes. On one course at Henley there were two *companies* with five members and six with six members. The two five-member *companies* finished first and second. On another course three five-member *companies* finished fifth, seventh, and eighth but in these instances the *companies* contained members who had not taken the tests – a sign associated for some reason with an unfavourable prognosis, (see Chapter Seven). There were other scattered five-member *companies* over the years but not in sufficient numbers to indicate any decisive advantage over teams comprising six members. What can be said is that five-man companies tended on the whole to be well-regulated *companies*. If they had the talent, they made good use of what they had.

Dangers of too small a team

If a chairman holds an easy balance in a five-man team, could he not do so with equal distinction in a three-man team? Is not a three-man team the shining example of a compact group offering the maximum in the way of involvement for its members?

It is interesting to speculate on how three-man teams might have fared pitted against those with four, five or six members. We have no real evidence as to what might have been achieved. What does seem apparent is that the 'chairman' of such a team would be something of a misnomer, if by the term chairman we mean someone who is skilled in using the resources of the group. The chairman of a three-man team would have more in common with a one-man team than with a chairman of a five-man team. In other words he is close to being a boss with two subordinates.

Three men of high ability and complementary skills could become very effective if they act in unison. However the word team now becomes only marginally relevant. The point about a team is that it enjoys a life of its own. Its membership may change but it still continues. Its authority does not depend on or demand the presence of any single individual. The same cannot be said for a three-man team. Decisions are inextricably linked with personalities and if one person is absent, business cannot continue without the risk of seriously changing the line that might otherwise have been taken.

A political example of a three-man team was demonstrated in Russia after the rejection of the 'cult of personality'. The favoured troika kept the chairman of the Politburo, the Prime Minister, and the Party Secretary in harness. It formed a halfway house between a dictatorship and management by a full team, having some of the advantages of both. Other countries have produced their own troikas which in their particular versions make for a more streamlined and consistent form of management than a Prime Minister and a cabinet of between 12 and 20 ministers.

Industrial examples of troikas usually rest on the relationships established between the Company Chairman (or in the U.S. the Corporation President), the Managing Director, and the (operational) General Manager. Often, major decisions are taken by these three in the first place and later ratified by a management executive or the board. In both political and industrial cases an essential feature of the troika is that each of its members has responsibilities that span the whole field. Because a troika member is not responsible for a department or ministry he can concentrate on developing his Team Role relationships with the other two members and is not impeded by limited responsibilities to push a particular set of interests that may run counter to what best serves the firm or the system as a whole.

Three members, as we have observed, may make for stable policy but they also make a team vulnerable. Even the smallest changes may affect its cohesion. Reducing bigness has the effect of magnifying the uncertainties that attach to particular personalities. As we proceed down the scale of team size we inevitably reach a crossover point where the team is no longer a team as such but an individual with supporters. When that happens any decisions that are taken tend to last only so long as that leading individual is around. Therein lies the weakness of autocrats, even benevolent autocrats. As soon as death intervenes or the throne becomes vacant for whatever cause, the empire or firm changes direction and character. The emphasis which dominated a leader's thinking for years becomes negated within a few months or even weeks. If we are thinking about real life, rather than management games, then the trio, we may suggest, is the point at which the team runs up against the risk of being too small to withstand later challenge. If we are thinking about efficiency, then the composition of the trio leaves no margin for error.

From what has been said, the ideal size of a team is a matter of compromise between conflicting forces. On the one hand there is a need to widen the composition, bringing in the full range of knowledge, experience, and ability. The wishes of individuals or representatives to participate through consultation or the political desirability of securing commitment of all departments are amongst the many pressures that operate to inflate numbers. Yet on the other hand there is the need to reduce noise and maximize involvement and individual effectiveness by keeping the team small.

Team size and the environment

There are certain factors in the physical environment which can also have a bearing on ideal team size. This was brought home to us at Henley. The stately home which the College occupies contains rooms of unequal dimensions. Nor is the furniture standard; in particular the tables vary in size and shape, some being of moderate dimensions while others seem designed for conferences. A conference table in a room of moderate size had the effect of minimizing movement around the table. One member of a team would be less likely to go round to the other side to confer with another. Less use was made of visual aids and charts on free-standing boards.

The shape of the table also had a bearing on the way in which the team operated. A Chairman sitting at the head of a long rectangular table was inclined to run his or her company in a strictly formal fashion, whereas those seated around a square or nearly square table acted like members of a peer group.

Tables and rooms have an important bearing on the social organisation of management. In spite of this many firms underestimate the need for meeting rooms and give little thought to their specification. The result is that there is usually nothing available between the standard office, which is too small, and one full conference room, which is vast.

Teams expand so as to fill the rooms available to hold them. Teams then become ideal for the rooms but not for the purpose for which they are set up. Conversely teams shrink in membership to fit into available offices, thereby creating the impression, not unjustifiably, that major decisions are taken by small cliques.

If firms and institutions are to recognize the importance and potential of well-balanced teams, they must provide rooms and tables that are ideal for their use. It is better to build a room to suit the needs of the ideal team than to modify the composition of the team in the interests of fitting it into the room.

Summary

■ The bigger the group, the greater the pressure towards conformity.

■ Teams of 10 worked for the Romans, but not for business.

■ Teams have an optimum size.

■ Environmental factors influence inter-personal behaviour.

Chapter 10

Features of good members of a team

Into the ark the managers went two by two. There were two types of negotiator (Resource Investigator [RI] and Team Worker [TW]), manager-worker (Implementer [IMP] and Completer Finisher [CF]), intellectual (Monitor Evaluator [ME] and Plant [PL]), and team leader (Co-ordinator [CO] and Shaper [SH]). These ark members in all the various combinations of characteristics provide the basic material for populating the whole world of management teams. The RI is the creative negotiator; the TW, the internal facilitator; the IMP, the effective organiser; the CF, the one who guarantees delivery; the ME, the analyser of problems; the PL, the source of original solutions; the CO, the team controller; and the SH, the slave-driver (where something stronger than control is needed). Management teams thrive on having members who are good examples of these types.

The diversity of personalities needed for a team raises the question therefore of whether those who are suitable have anything in common. Are there features that distinguish the effective team member, where the member can be defined as someone who readily finds a fitting part to play in the context of the team and always makes himself useful?

For many years during our experimental work we depended on observers to produce objective records of individual behaviour in teams. During the latter part of our studies we invited our observers to pick out individuals who in their opinion had made the most valuable contributions to the performance of the group. They were also asked to expand on how this had been achieved. There would have been a scientific advantage in asking them also to pick out the person who had contributed least or who had detracted most from the achievement of the group so that comparison might be made, but this we thought politically inadvisable. Some observers did spontaneously comment on members who in their view had been passengers in the team. In the main we built up a knowledge of effective team members in terms of their positive qualities in an absolute sense rather than by comparison with poor team members. In any case, we had plenty of examples of the latter from our own case study experience.

Contribution and team role

Those identified as contributing most to team performance were drawn from the ranks of all the key Team Roles. Marginally at the head of the list were those with Plant and Implementer characteristics. Next on the list were Chairman-type members, but only if these did at some stage secure the role of Chairman. Here several triumphs were scored by those who were not originally elected to take the chair but who came to the fore when the *company* was floundering and the members voted for job changes which in effect produced a new leadership. If that *company* then performed well, the person in charge was often given the major share of the credit. His job would be that of chairman but his Team Role type would be different, approximating most closely to that of, say, Team Worker. Such a Chairman would foster a good team spirit and produce the climate in which the group could flourish. The greater the signs of early interpersonal difficulties, the more such a member was appreciated. Generally for a person to receive strong mention as a contributor it was necessary for the group to get into some sort of difficulty from which it could be rescued by the member with the abilities and personal qualities commensurate with the task. A mention would not necessarily imply that a nominated member was in essence an outstanding team member: it could be no more than that he/she was well suited to a particular situation. What was more convincing was when mention was combined with a description of the member's skills so that these stood out as impressive in their own right.

From the sample of cases built up in this way, a good team player was seen to transcend Team Role. A good member could adjust to a situation that called for a Team Role he/she did not possess and yet he/she could still maintain his/her personal effectiveness. On the other hand, someone with one strong Team Role characteristic could be an asset to a team when matters flowed naturally in his/her direction but a liability as soon as his/her particular strength was no longer demanded by the situation. The late Charles de Gaulle would be an example of the latter. An example of the former might be the late Chou En-lai, Prime Minister during much of the Mao Tse-tung era, who succeeded in keeping the ship of state afloat whether in the waters on which a 100 flowers were blooming or amid the turbulence of the Cultural Revolution. While good members of a team vary in their natural abilities and Team Roles, there are certain generalizations that can be offered about them.

Timing

Outstanding team members have an ability to time their interventions. They seem able to judge the moment that is ripe for their emergence in the particular Team Role in which they are able to contribute effectively. The rider is that they know when to keep silent. The silent phase is not a passive one in which they are 'switched off'; because, it is only by the maintenance of attention and interest during the silent phase that they can judge the moment at which their own contribution is likely to be most appreciated. Typically neither the compulsive talker nor the shy introvert possesses this type of capacity for timing. For the compulsive talker every moment is the one ripe for personal intervention; for the shy introvert the moment at which to intervene is governed by occasional surges in self-confidence rather than the objective needs of the situation.

CASE STUDY – A DOMINANT TEAM MEMBER WHO OVERTALKED

The importance of timing was well illustrated in a negative way by a certain Reg Scorer, a man of very wide experience. His test scores revealed particularly high mental ability and creative disposition. He was also strong in dominance and low in anxiety. Scorer appreciated the value of teams and declared great interest in the whole

Continued

field of group psychology, which he could easily back up with appropriate quotations from published research.

On first meeting, Scorer's talents immediately commended themselves. After that reactions to him varied. Some people would maintain an amicable relationship, while others cooled rapidly. Within a team however, it became evident that team members collectively learnt to gang up against him. His knowledge, wide experience and ideas tempted him to overplay his hand at every opportunity. A display of resistance in the form of scepticism merely stimulated him to redouble his efforts in marshalling his arguments, finding supporting evidence for his ideas and rebutting objectors. There seemed almost no subject that was immune to his winning points. Eventually Scorer found himself being boycotted. Information was withheld from him. Arguments were manufactured to be used against him. This seemed to become even more important than the pursuit of the collective goal.

Even more remarkable than the conspiracy that Scorer seemed to provoke against him was his failure to perceive the gathering indifference, and then hostility, that his behaviour engendered. Undisguised boredom, even yawning, did nothing to diminish the flowing wisdom that poured from his lips. To his credit he responded to the eventually poor performance of his team with some magnanimity, being only too ready to blame himself for various oversights and mistakes. In fact Scorer's strategies on how problems should be tackled were basically sound. His prime misfortune was that others worked so badly in any team of which he was a member.

Plants generally figure amongst the most successful as well as the least successful members. It could be that PLs need a good back-up role, such as that of TW or ME. This brings us to the second feature that characterizes the effective team member: the ability to switch flexibly between different Team Roles.

Flexibility

One leading industrialist, on the Boards of an exceptionally large number of companies, declared that he played a slightly different role in each company. Whether that was so or not could not be confirmed. We could, however, build up a dossier of authenticated material on one industrialist who rose eventually to the apex of managerial responsibility in a nationalized industry, and who was well known for his distinctive style of management.

CASE STUDY – A SUCCESSFUL MANAGER WITH REAL FLEXIBILITY

Mervyn Hawley joined a large process industry as a young man having reputedly walked into the town, where a large factory offered many opportunities for employment, carrying all that he possessed with him. Mervyn was soon recognized for his enterprise and initiative and gradually climbed the ladder of responsibility until his own lack of qualifications became the main barrier to further advancement. At this point he decided to study for a degree in an appropriate technical subject while continuing his job. After his graduation he advanced rapidly within the organisation, bypassing in promotion older graduates holding better degrees gained in the most prestigious universities, until he eventually found himself in command of tens of thousands of people.

Mervyn showed unusual skill in getting the most out of any team of which he was a member. Here his typical pattern involved three phases of operation. The first phase was the preparation of the ground. During this phase he had a habit of wandering about tracking down information to its sources. Wearing a white overall, he would mingle with the shift workers, usually being taken for a laboratory assistant. Men asked for their views on issues connected with their work or questioned on points of work detail are only too happy to supply the answers if they are approached in the right way. Mervyn would arrive at meetings better prepared than his colleagues. At these meetings he was reluctant to declare what he already knew but instead favoured an informal discussion which gradually turned into a free-for-all. This second phase was a feet up on the table affair with any differences in rank or status totally ignored. Just when the possibilities and options seemed endless, the second phase would end. Feet would come off the table, rank and authority reasserted themselves. Mervyn would make a decision and from then on it would be Mr. Hawley, the driving force, who would turn decision into unrelenting action.

Hawley's ability to interchange the Team Roles of TW, RI, and Shaper (SH) gave him a repertoire that fitted him well for a wide range of managerial situations. Nevertheless a change in Team Role is not easy to bring about convincingly. Those who are capable of sudden switches need to signify to their colleagues which Team Role they are now adopting. Dress and body language both have a part to play in this: some managers take off their jackets in discussion with colleagues when they need to dispense with the pressures and constraints that attach to rank and authority; equally they invoke them by returning to formality in dress when the occasion demands. Experienced managers find various means of signifying their Team Role intentions. Spectacles can be put away to allow for more intimate eye-to-eye contact and to encourage communication; the lenses can be wiped to signify contemplation of the issues in question; or spectacles can be worn, even if there is no need for their normal usage in reading as a means of focusing the attention of the group on the gravity of the decision-making moment. In one large manufacturing establishment the Chief Executive wore a pair of pince-nez spectacles that he used in a flexible way to good effect for establishing the appropriate cues in role relationships. His ocular accoutrements were copied by other managers but although pince-nez became an emblem of management, other managers failed to use them to the same good purpose!

Self-restraint

If managers have more than one part to play in teams they will need to establish clearly the Team Roles they intend to adopt, but they will also need to decide which Team Roles they are *not* going to play. By limiting their own Team Role ranges, they provide the opportunity for others to develop their own distinctive capabilities and in doing so the group is strengthened by the sense of community and common purpose that is produced by interdependence of effort. Some managers are as remarkable for what they refrain from doing as for what they do. The importance of this restraint is easily underestimated.

CASE STUDY – A SUCCESSFUL LOW-PROFILE CO-ORDINATOR

Peter Pointer was Chairman of a large industrial group, having attained the position at an unusually early age. But Pointer was not a bright young whiz kid. Had others tried to model themselves on his apparent behaviour it would have been difficult to do so since there was not a great deal of overt management style that was available for imitation. The meetings over which he presided were well conducted. In the chair he made fewer interventions than the average intervention rate of others attending the same meeting. What distinguished Pointer's own contribution was his capacity to sum up. The summing up was not always a balanced account of what had gone beforehand but it did represent a judicious conclusion and verdict on the proceedings that no one ever challenged. In spite of Pointer's low contribution rate, as judged by volume, the meetings over which he presided had a reputation for solid achievement.

Using team role voids to advantage

Self-imposed restraint is one way of opening up the field for others and so giving scope for the group to explore its latent resources. A more deliberate and sophisticated way of doing this is to create a Team Role void, which another is then invited to fill. The skilful team player will build up a specification of what is needed within the team if some important task is to be accomplished but declare a personal lack of qualification or skill for the task. The stronger the self-declaration of an inability to enter the role, the more powerful becomes the invitation to others to rise to the occasion. By acting in this way a good team player stands in contrast to the typical careerist who is usually anxious to display his full range of skills at every opportunity. Yet the former often overtakes the latter in the promotion stakes because he/she builds up such strong support amongst colleagues.

CASE STUDY – CREATING A VOID FOR OTHERS TO FILL

A striking example of this type of team-orientated approach was once told to me by an industrial executive recounting his experience in the navy. He had the good fortune as a young man in the services to work closely with an admiral. It soon became apparent to him that the admiral's management style contrasted with the pattern of styles that he had encountered amongst other officers in the navy. The initial impression was that the admiral was poorly endowed with grey matter. Instead of acting as the wise arbiter and decision-maker on all matters referred to him, which is what might be expected of an admiral, difficult problems were always referred to the clever young men on his staff. These young men busied themselves in furnishing the admiral with reports, graphs, and tables of figures in support of any opinion that they chose to offer when consulted. The admiral commonly reacted to the merest overload of information or hint of ambiguity with bewilderment. He would declare that he could not understand what a report meant. If it was possible to misinterpret a table of figures he would do so. Occasionally graphs would be held upside down. The bright young men learnt to respond by writing more concise reports, marshalling their arguments better, and separating relevant from irrelevant data. The decisions taken, like all other matters connected with the admiral, had a habit of turning out well. In due course my informant had concluded that the admiral was not the stupid old buffoon he had originally mistaken him for, that he had a sharply critical mind, and that, above all, he had developed a fine technique for handling and developing a team of bright young men.

Maintaining team goals

The skilled member sets up others in appropriate Team Roles for which he/she prepares the ground by creating a void into which they can enter. Clearly this approach can appeal to managers for different reasons. Letting others do the work does offer respite from personal effort and responsibility. The difference between exploiting other team members and developing them may not always be easy to discern; but it is important. Team success depends to a great extent on having members who set team goals above those of personal self-interest. The manager who is team-motivated will set up a role for others because it serves the wider purpose of the team and not for any ulterior motive. There are occasions when a job that needs to be done in a team is shirked by everyone within it. In that case the manager who places the interests of the team above his personal inclination to engage or not engage in a particular piece of behaviour will himself step into the breach. In other words, the characteristics of good team players lie not so much in the jobs that they do or do not do but in the flexible ways in which they adapt their behaviour to cope with the needs of situations. Here they must learn to judge the capabilities of each member of the team in relation to the jobs to be done, treating themselves on the same basis as others.

Some brave team members distinguish themselves by their readiness to engage in undertakings that others avoid. They intervene merely because a job needs doing.

CASE STUDY – AN ABILITY TO GRASP THE NETTLE

One manager with a great capacity for taking on unpopular jobs was Fred Blunt, the Works Manager of a large steel complex. Fred was a Yorkshireman who had risen from the ranks, furthering his education at night school during his rise through the middle echelons of management. Now, in the upper councils of the corporation, Fred contrasted with his colleagues in personality, outlook and abilities. His colleagues had mostly enjoyed successful university careers followed by the company's investment in their career development; they had been moved from one post to the next and from one regional location to another in a logically conceived widening of their experience and responsibilities. Fred, on the other hand, was the local boy made good. No one had planned that he should reach his present appointment. It had just happened, though no one regretted it. Fred was certainly not intellectual but he had an inimitable way of coping with people and situations. He was regarded as an asset in a management team even by colleagues who crossed swords with him at regular intervals.

On one occasion the company was beset with an industrial relations problem that had persisted for an unacceptably long period. The managers concerned met to discuss how the problem might be resolved. In due course it became apparent that Spinks, the industrial relations officer most directly concerned with the affair, had not handled matters too cleverly. This was surprising since Spinks was a youngish university graduate quite able in his way, though evidently moved by sentiment and idealism rather than judgment. Once Spinks's mistakes had been catalogued it became evident that he was the weak link in the chain. He would have to be moved but there was no obvious position into which to move him. A temporary post might be found but the best solution was to get him to leave the company, which should cause him no great problem as he was, on paper, very marketable. With the exception of Fred, the managers at this meeting demurred at this solution. It would be too sudden. It might be seen as unfair. On the other hand it would be the ideal way out. "Has anybody told Spinks he has done a bad job?", asked Fred. The answers were vague and indefinite. No one had exactly told him. There had been several hints. It was very difficult. He always appeared pleasant and responsive when suggestions were made to him but nothing really changed. "Does he know that he has not done a good job?" said Fred. Further equivocations followed. "Right," said Fred, "call Spinks to my office. I'll see him now." That same day Spinks called at the Works Manager's office and by mutual arrangement his career with the company was terminated.

Fred Blunt was an amenable, popular manager, but unflinching whenever a difficult human situation had to be faced. Character counts whenever an important job lacks takers. In one case what is needed is moral courage; in another, exacting self-discipline; or in yet another, a readiness to endure tedium. A willingness to make a personal but well-judged sacrifice in the corporate interest is the mark of an effective SH. The mere wish to belong to social groups is often mistaken for and has little in common with this quality.

In conclusion, effective team membership can be viewed as something that transcends fitness for any particular Team Role. Those who are nominated by others as 'good to have in a team' have an ability to time their interventions, to vary their role, to limit their contributions, to create roles for others and to do some of the jobs that others deliberately avoid. Whether these tendencies amount to skills or whether they are qualities of character is a moot point. The simple fact is that the natural teamsman is very likely to be enrolled into a team, even with the minimum of credentials, because he is seen as someone who pulls his weight and does nothing to detract from the contribution of others. Those who are organising and composing teams may usefully pay as much attention to a candidate's teamsmanship as to any specialized ability he may possess.

Summary

- Certain Team Roles can form a natural pair.
- Effective team members know how to time their interventions.
- Good team members create opportunities for others.
- Good managers show strength of character in facing reality.

Chapter 11

Designing a team

Management teams are commonly made up of members holding particular appointments. They are there by virtue of the offices or responsibilities they represent. No overall sense of design governs the composition of the group which, in human terms, is little more than a random collection of senior managers with as wide a spread of human foibles and personality characteristics as one might expect to find in the population at large. Nevertheless what we have established, or endeavoured to establish in this book, is that the compatibility of members of the management team is crucial to its effectiveness. It is a subject of no less importance than whether members of a team are talented as accountants, production engineers, or salesmen. The problem is that human compatibility is more difficult to assess than technical competence. Our experiments and fieldwork have given leads on how the subject of compatibility within the management team might be approached. Methods and techniques will vary but some fundamentals remain unchanged. To guide us in our work of team design, five interlocking principles can be set out:

1. Members of a management team can contribute in two ways to the achievement of team objectives. They can perform well in a functional role in drawing on their professional and technical knowledge as the situation demands. They also have a potentially valuable Team Role to perform. A Team Role describes a pattern of behaviour characteristic of the way in which one team member interacts with others in facilitating the progress of the team.

2. Each team needs an optimum balance in both functional roles and Team Roles. The ideal blend will depend on the goals and tasks the team faces.

3. The effectiveness of a team will be promoted by the extent to which members correctly recognize and adjust themselves to the relative strengths within the team both in expertise and ability to engage in specific Team Roles.

4. Personal qualities fit members for some Team Roles while limiting the likelihood that they will succeed in others.

5. A team can deploy its technical resources to best advantage only when it has the requisite range of Team Roles to ensure efficient teamwork.

Obtaining information

Acquiring reliable data about people is the starting point for effective team building. Some thought therefore needs to be given as to how this may be done. The approach on which we mainly relied was the battery of psychometric tests, including some we had developed ourselves with the specific purpose of gaining the data we needed on Team Role disposition and abilities. Some large companies well equipped with resources use comparable methods. The favoured approach is to collect the required information about people at the time of recruitment. This not only enables a firm to make a more informed decision as to whether a particular candidate should be taken on but also provides a data bank with good storage life offering a number of prospective uses: for example, the information can be used as an aid to career development. Individuals can be moved into positions where they are likely to fulfil themselves because their Team Role capabilities fit the situation.

Another way of obtaining data on the Team Role capabilities of intending team members is to use in-company training courses. Course participants learn about assessment methods and about those principles that govern the effectiveness of management teams. As they will wish to experience what is involved they are invited to complete two questionnaires on Team Role, one based on self-perception (a form of this is given on pp. 178–83) and the other relating to the perceived Team Role capabilities of known fellow participants. The information can then be used to form experimental teams on the training course. If the experience is rewarding, participants may agree that the information has a constructive value and can be used in a wider setting to compose or recompose management groups or project teams. Clearly this can only happen where mutual trust prevails and when individuals are satisfied that any discrepancies regarding their personal Team Roles have been satisfactorily sorted out.

Sophisticated methods and procedures are not, however, indispensable for forming well-integrated teams. Many firms evaluate their executives in annual assessments for the purpose of management planning and development. In other cases managers feel they know enough already about the people who report to them. What is lacking is not a sufficiency of information on the strengths, weaknesses and managing styles of those at the nucleus of the enterprise, but rather a tactical line on how to make better use of the information already available. Managers conversant with Team Role theory have mentioned two ways in which they have changed their approach on simple, everyday issues.

Recruitment

The first reported benefit relates to recruitment. When a new manager is being sought, what sort of person should the company look for? The orthodox, almost reflex response, is for a company to search for someone who fits the image of those who are already there. Fewer problems then arise in mutual adjustment between the newcomer and his established colleagues. But as we have already seen, the fact that assimilation is free of complications does not mean that the person being assimilated corresponds with what the organisation needs. In Team Role terms the more fundamental need is for someone who will fill the Team Role gap in management. This cannot be ascertained without completing a Team Role inventory of colleagues and examining what is missing. Once this is done a specification can be drawn up of the general shape of the candidate the firm would like to recruit. The interview now becomes directed towards the key question that the selectors will be posing to themselves: how well does the candidate match the personal specification?

Internal reshuffling

The second immediate benefit of using Team Role concepts relates to internal postings. Managers have reported advantages in being able to make bolder moves than they would otherwise contemplate through confidence that the appointee will contribute to the Team Role that is lacking. This occurs typically where the experience that the incoming manager brings with him is not altogether appropriate but his natural orientation and behaviour more than compensates for any presumed deficiency in technical knowledge. The converse point is also reported as being important: internal postings that suggested themselves for technical reasons have been cancelled once the unpromising implications of the move in Team Role terms have been explored.

In these negative instances, success cannot be claimed because no one can prove that mistakes have been avoided. It is easier to see errors of judgment in retrospect by re-examining cases where considerations of experience and technical competence have dominated the question of transfer to the exclusion of interpersonal considerations.

The danger of destroying partnerships

A common mistake is to underestimate the dynamic factors that bind together the smallest team of all. Pairings of proven effectiveness are often broken up to fill managerial gaps or even as well-intentioned acts of management development, with little realization of how much the interdependence of two people contributes to the running of a successful unit. At one stage in my industrial career I witnessed an episode that had much to teach on the importance of these one-to-one relationships.

CASE STUDY – THE BREAK-UP OF AN EFFECTIVE PARTNERSHIP

O'Hara first came to my notice as the man running the office of a large production department in a company engaged in the extrusion and fabrication of plastics. One day the post of the manager of the department became vacant unexpectedly, the culmination, it must be said, of a number of production crises and turmoil that the department had been through. During this time one man had come to the fore as the only person who had made much progress in remedying the machine faults and effectively stemming the rise of scrap due to recurrent problems. Sims was one of the fitters in the tool room. True, he had been spotted before. In the preceding year the tool room manager had been away ill and Sims had been put temporarily in charge. The experiment had not been a success, for Sims had merely carried on with his usual work and only involved himself with others in the tool room when pushed into doing so. It was a great relief when the tool room manager had returned. Nevertheless someone had to be put in charge of the department and with no other candidates in view a choice had to be made between O'Hara and Sims. The dilemma was whether to pick someone who was technically underqualified but skilful with people or to go for the most technically able man who had shown not the slightest inkling of management ability.

After much thought the job was offered, though not without some misgivings, to O'Hara. O'Hara accepted but did so on the condition that Silent Sims, as he was known to some, should be transferred to the department as the technical foreman. This was granted. The department now settled down to those familiar problems with which it had been long beset before the vacancy had arisen. However, within a few months all those indices that management uses to monitor efficiency began to register progress. This was remarkable since O'Hara and Sims had been part of the environment during those previous years when seemingly endless difficulties had been experienced.

The two men now struck up a close association and friendship within the department, while outside the department O'Hara was active in developing those contacts that extended his scope in the job. As time went on O'Hara forged links with the top rank of the company, frequently attending executive meetings. There, his natural fluency, unusual for works personnel, general charm, and sense of intimate knowledge about what was happening on the shop floor made a considerable impression. Only when it came to discussing options on unprepared ground did O'Hara become hesitant. He always wanted time to consult colleagues when conversation moved on to technical matters or complex policy issues.

Expansion of the business at last opened up the possibility of setting up a new automatic product line at Asheville, a factory some 15 miles away. O'Hara was nominated as factory manager. It seemed a natural choice. O'Hara was jubilant but put in a plea that Sims should come with him as technical manager. Unfortunately for O'Hara, Sims was considered indispensable where he was: he could have anybody else but Sims. This news seemed to depress O'Hara, but once over it and having adjusted to the inevitable, he set about organising the new factory with his characteristic vigour.

Eighteen months elapsed before I had an occasion to visit the company again and could inquire how our two friends were faring. Sadly, their fortunes had risen only to fall. O'Hara had been quite unsuccessful as a factory manager, failing to get on top of any of the real problems. He was brought back to base as the Assistant Production Manager only to lose his job as part of a general cutback. Sims was still there, troubleshooting on a new line, but no longer operating as a supervisor. The once flourishing partnership was dead, buried, and long forgotten.

Successful twosomes are more stable in top management than on the way up. A Chairman and a Managing Director who establish a good working relationship maintain it to the benefit of the enterprise as a whole. In contrast, any junior executive pair that does well will seldom be seen as anything other than two able individuals. Higher authorities will decide their respective destinies as they find themselves shunted into groups that are sometimes viable, sometimes not. Since role relationships are not readily discernible, they are likely to be ignored whenever career progression is being considered.

Sims and O'Hara, while their partnership lasted, could have formed the nucleus of a good team. But once their separation has taken place, which poses the more challenging problem in placement. Most personnel men would be drawn to O'Hara as the senior man. But where the purpose is to bring about effective team building, Sims might make the greater claim for closer personnel attention. The argument is as follows: if managers possess general skills in being able to manage people, functions and businesses, it follows that they are more interchangeable than the specialists who report to them: good managers can be freely moved around and do not pose a major placement problem. That being so, it can become a better strategy to make a priority of finding a first-rate technical man for a department where technical factors are critical and then to find the manager who is most likely to fit in with him.

Sequence of selection

This reversal of normal practice is the way in which we built up our most successful winning teams in the EME. We would start with an especially clever and creative individual or Superplant. Having selected him we then moved on to pick someone who would make a good team leader. The analogy in the world beyond management games is to look in the first place for a man of super talent in his field rather than for a manager.

Suppose a major new public building is to be erected, and is to be not only functional, but also at the same time be a monument of its kind. The first step is to search for an outstanding architect. Or take the case of a company that needs to build a special purpose machine to a demanding specification for its own internal use, but which could recover its development cost by serving a wider market outside the firm. Then it becomes necessary to find a design engineer of distinction before any further steps are contemplated. After that we may consider, in both cases, our next move – how the project shall be managed.

An alternative to the steps advocated would be to commission a consulting company dealing with architecture or with engineering design. This must be seen as second best. A company may only be as good as its stars. The experience may be not dissimilar to going back to a hotel renowned for its cuisine, only to find that its talented chef had left 6 months earlier. No company that supplies a service can be taken on faith until one knows more about the talents of the key person who, in the last analysis, will be most intimately connected with meeting the needs of the client.

If we revert to the project within the firm, the proposal to pick the best specialist or the most suitable genius to begin with, and to follow this with choice of a project leader, is open to the objection that, providing the sequence is not made public, one ends up with the same people anyway. The selection of A to be accompanied by B gives us the same pairing as starting with B and attaching to him A. To some the sequence in decision making is seen as being immaterial to the decisions ultimately made. This we find to be as untrue as the notion that if two moves are to be made in chess it matters little which is played first.

Design and purpose

Let us consider two types of team built for different purposes, each to contain five members. One team is needed to design a new model and prepare a prototype. Another is needed to streamline the system destined to produce it. In the case of the former, a designer of genius may be required. Such a man would require someone of equal intellectual acumen, whom he can respect, to monitor him and keep him under control. A good candidate for the job is found but neither he nor the designer look like managers. We now have to find a manager to 'chair' the project, who will adopt a low profile and give those with the ability their heads. The favoured nominee has the personal controlling power to take on someone else under his wing. So, further one person with creative talents, complementary to those of the first nominee, and a wide range of contacts seems worth enlisting. This last member is an acceptable person who is likely to work well with others but happens to be weak in follow up. This conditions the choice of the final member as a person with solid organising ability who is also a meticulous finisher. The resulting well-balanced team, depicted with our Team Role notation, is shown as Team I and can be compared in its composition with Team II. Here the emphasis switches away from the management of innovation towards getting things done at high speed in a politically sensitive area.

A design format for two five-man teams

Team I

Co-ordinator/Team Worker

| Superplant | Monitor-Evaluator/Implementer |
| Resource Investigator/Team Worker | Implementer/Completer-Finisher |

Team II

	Shaper/Completer-Finisher	
Monitor Evaluator/Team Worker	Team Worker/Implementer
Implementer/Team Worker	Completer-Finisher/Team Worker

For Team I, richly endowed with talent and resources, the problem of management is primarily one of controlling the balance with no more than the occasional, though firm, touch on the tiller. Team II, on the other hand, calls for leadership from the front. Someone with relentless drive, who can be guaranteed to get results and ensure that schedules are met, is appointed. The group that is set up for this streamlining/organising project is essentially a support team around a leader. Each member is likely to possess skills that will compensate for and cover the team leader's bulldozing ability, while having something positive, probably of a technical nature, to contribute in his own right. Members of Team II are rather more similar to one another than members of Team I, but in the circumstances that is inevitable. Had our leader been depicted as belonging to the Shaper/Team Worker type, an unlikely but not impossible combination here, there would seem less merit in constructing a support team. Other Team Roles might have been introduced which would have had the effect of offering more competition with the leader from within the team.

Creating teams from working groups

The question of the interaction of members within a team becomes more important the more often a team meets. But what happens when a team meets only rarely? Everyone is busy doing his own particular job and it is the interplay of work that constitutes the team effort rather than the effectiveness in combination when the members convene as a group. Now the likelihood of role clashes diminishes but the question of Team Role coverage remains just as important. Members of a team will be assigned separate tasks consistent with their Team Role characteristics and they will meet formally only when the tasks are done or near completion.

It is evident that people may work as a team without being part of a working group. Conversely people may belong to the same working group without constituting a team. The essence of a team is that its members form a co-operative association through a division of labour that best reflects the contribution that each can make towards the common objective. The members do not need to be present at the same place and at the same time to enable the team to function.

Good teams would be much easier to form in industry for project work or management meetings if thought were given to the Team Role composition of natural working groups. In practice there are a multitude of reasons why well-balanced teams are unlikely to form spontaneously. People are often picked for working groups because they are sensed as having characteristics akin to those who are already there, as discussed in Chapter Three. So redundancies in some Team Roles will be associated with shortages in others. At higher levels of responsibility similar Team Role types are found because the organisation favours and rewards with promotion those with particular styles of approach.

Teams in static structures

One of the prime obstacles is that a rigid hierarchical structure precludes entry into the team of the most suitable individuals. This raises the question of how a good team can be formed in an organisation that is not recruiting or likely to transfer people from the jobs they currently hold.

The suggested approach here is to avoid building teams on the basis of *ex officio* appointments. A meeting of heads of departments, for example, can all too easily turn into a gathering of Shapers with disastrous results. It is often better to set up a project or study team following the principles of team design drawing on people at different levels in the hierarchy. Such a team will not have the same authority as one drawn from functional heads of the organisation but it is likely to be more effective. What is then needed, however, is a way of relating the project team to the organisation so that its work may gain the backing of the organisation as a whole, for the project will have little standing in its own right. Where the members of a project team are not nominees of departments but the appointees of whoever forms the team, there is a political as well as a consulting need to involve heads of departments. The most convenient way of doing this is to convene a project steering group that will meet occasionally and briefly advise the project team on guidelines and objectives. The reporting structure can allow each team to report to the Chief Executive. By this means, the ideally constituted project team is assured of its independence; it cannot be killed by any members of the hierarchy who are wedded to existing practice.

Establishing the right climate in which well-designed teams can form and flourish is the foundation stone on which more effective teamwork in the future can be built. Only then does it become possible to explore the many questions raised by trying to create an optimum combination of people. The merits of each potential member can be raised in terms of what technically he can contribute and the role that he is likely to play in the group that is being formed. Once this process starts, one finds that some people have more to contribute than others irrespective of what it is they have to offer. Designing a team engenders a search for individuals who are good examples of their type. A creative member needs to be very creative rather than moderately so; a tidy-minded, reliable individual may be appreciated for good finishing qualities but rather less so than someone of restrained disposition with a compulsive need to get things done.

Designing a team rests on a limited number of principles and concepts and involves various methods and techniques. But what turns team-building into an art is that the bricks, like legendary men, are made of different types of clay and not wholly predictable after firing.

Summary

- Selecting an ideal team is difficult, given that most teams are inherited.
- Recruitment can be facilitated by identifying the missing Team Roles.
- Successful partnerships should not be broken up without due cause, since they rely on the complementary abilities of both people.
- The Team Role balance should be appropriate to the objectives of the work.

Chapter 12

Teams in
public affairs

The last experiment in our joint programme of work with Henley in composing management teams was sober and subdued. This seems to be what happens when wonder ceases, the expected comes to pass, and the moment for departure arrives. We had learned much about the problems in putting a team together and how to overcome them. We thought the time was ripe to disseminate the message.

As we proceeded in this direction we came across a growing number of interested parties in the area of public administration. Here was a dilemma. Our experience had been largely founded on experimentally formed companies competing against each other to achieve a financial outcome. Measuring this outcome gave us a yardstick of effectiveness.

On one hand, what we had learned seemed most appropriate to private enterprise and less applicable to non-commercial objectives. On the other hand, there was the view that the financial outcome was no more than a convenient means of measuring team effectiveness.

The success or failure of these teams depended on certain principles. Could the lessons derived from them be put to good use in the management of public affairs? Such an approach might entail examining the key areas in the planning and decision-making process; ensuring that individuals with key skills got into teams of the right size where their abilities could be used to advantage; and training selectors in methods for forming teams with an adequate Team Role balance (amongst the other balances that would also need to be taken into account). If that task were undertaken rigorously, government might operate more efficiently whether at a national or a local level.

Structure and power in government

Such an approach would be easy in principle if government had a clear-cut management structure and a simple reporting system. But it does not. In comparison with industry, public affairs in democratic society suffer not only from the drawback of being inherently more complicated but also from being conducted in a less orderly fashion. The onlooker is often uncertain as to where the vital decisions are made and this uncertainty usually is not far from the reality.

Aneurin Bevan, the Welsh politician responsible for founding the National Health Service, saw his life as a politician as a journey in search of the place where real power lay; and declared at the end that he never found it.

We were reminded of the elusive nature and locus of power and responsibility during a visit to Canberra during our studies. This trip followed an invitation to conduct a seminar on the running of management teams for the Public Service Board.

Canberra is one of the few purpose-built capitals of the world, originally no more than a small rural town before being transformed into a landscaped city of 200,000 people on a scale that does justice to the size of the Australian continent. This great centre of government seemed the obvious place in which we might find answers to our long-stored questions on public policy and strategies for coping with problems. These were problems that Australia has in common with other developed countries.

In spite of being personally taken round Canberra by a member of the Prime Minister's office and availing ourselves of introductions to many co-operative people, no answers were forthcoming about where real decision-making power lay, and we were referred instead to the State capitals from which we had already come.

This caused no surprise to our Australian colleagues. The image of government is of power emanating from a central core but the closer one gets to that core, the more amorphous it becomes. The purpose of this capital city was more difficult to envisage and appreciate by visiting it than by viewing if from afar.

Some may consider it a good thing that power with its corrupting influence is not concentrated too strongly at any one point. Deliberate avoidance of centralized authority, however, can create a kind of managerial vacuum. Matters that demand urgent attention lie beyond the scope of any given body or person, or even when they can be tackled they fall uncomfortably between departments, where established machinery finds it difficult to function efficiently.

Bigness creates its own problems which are familiar to most large organisations. But the government suffers from both largeness and complexity in that it rests on an uneasily poised partnership between representatives elected to public office and those for whom public service is a career. The conventional picture is that politicians present a competing set of choices to the electorate from which those who are successful receive, collectively, a mandate to govern; it is then up to the civil servants to turn policies into practical programmes. Who then are better able to form the ideal policy-making team?

Politicians and teams

Constitutionally, the reply must be the politicians if they are viewed as the senior members of the partnership and as acting in the role credited to them by the public. On this premise, let us consider how we could ever hope to end up with our basic requirements for success: that is, a policy-forming and decision-making management team of ideal size with a well-balanced distribution in Team Role capabilities amongst those who form the team.

Here we run into inevitable difficulties. Political practices are bounded by sets of well-established constraints. In the first place there is virtually nothing that can be done about unit size. The whole system is built upon a certain ratio between electors and elected. The constituency dimensions are fixed. The numbers who assemble in their council chambers are virtually constant. Each Parliament, Senate or Congress (or its equivalent in any country of the world) will comprise several hundred representatives.

In the United Kingdom there are over 600 members of Parliament. This number is about one hundred times bigger than the ideal for formulating the most well-conceived policies.

Conventions

Now the argument may be put forward that policies are authorized by Parliament but actually have their origins in party conventions. Here again familiar problems stand in the way of our requirements. The conventions themselves tend to be oversized and their agendas concentrate on traditional subjects that are treated in a general way. It is perhaps as well that this is so. Large meetings are not the place at which judgments can be reached on difficult issues. Quite apart from the matter of size, the mood of such meetings is seldom one which favours dispassionate analysis and balanced decision-taking.

Committees

Many important decisions are taken, it is true, in committee where the 'noise' problem associated with big meetings is partly overcome. Nevertheless, the committee is to some extent the microcosm of the whole. The problem of producing coherence in both argument and approach will be lessened but will still remain. The smaller group will make for more meaningful exchange of views but the prospects of a co-ordinated approach are hardly improved. Members of a political group or committee will retain their individualism; they are there to press a case or to give expression to a viewpoint with which they are associated in the wider world.

This pursuit of a special interest is incompatible with what a team requires. A team differs from a group in that it demands from its members personal adjustment in playing one of a limited number of parts that together form an effective pattern. People need to be structured into a team. In how many political groups or committees is there a structuring force or a selector to decide or to advise on what type of members are needed and what part they are to play?

Let us now put aside the question of how well policies are likely to be prepared before politicians enter office and consider instead the position that arises on their arrival. Here we may ask: what Team Roles are they likely to fulfil?

Direct evidence is lacking but there are at least some indications. We have only to consider how politicians are selected in the first place to realize what qualities they will bring with them.

Likely team roles of politicians

What governs politicians' rise to the political forefront is the ability to create a sense of mission, to kindle enthusiasm about the things that people value; it is the ability to project hopes, to sense and respond to the mood of the public; it is the ability to use persuasive skills and energy in getting things done over a wide-ranging field.

Here we have an evident specification for Shapers and Resource Investigators. Such people are likely to be highly extroverted and continuously on the go. They will be typically better at coping with emergencies and in responding to events in the short term than those in the long term. Sir Harold Wilson neatly encapsulated the temporal dimensions of the world in which politicians live: 'a week is a long time in politics'.

The inner qualities of politicians, the pressures to which they are subject and the circumstances in which they operate in day-to-day life are hardly conducive to membership of the small effective policy-making teams that we have in mind. It is easier to see them fulfilling themselves as guardians of the political process and as managing the political scene.

Civil servants in teams

That being so, let us turn to examine their partners in government. The test results of Civil Servants who attended Henley over the years brought out two general points: firstly, they tended to be similar to corporate planners in industry but differed from other industrial managers by being more introverted; and secondly, a good proportion scored well on the measures of mental ability. This latter point is in line with the stringency of the examinations that they are required to pass in order to enter the Civil Service in the first place.

These criteria help to set the scene for the two 'clever' Team Roles, Plant and Monitor Evaluator. Here again, as might be expected, these two Team Roles – and especially the latter – were well represented. Neither of these Team Roles would fit easily into the political scene. The creative ideas man is in danger of falling foul of the political consensus that binds a party together, whereas in the Civil Service he can be hidden away in a back room. The prospect of a political career looks no more promising for the classic Monitor Evaluator. Dry, dispassionate and slow-moving souls are not the stuff of which political candidates are made. Implementer and Team Worker Team Roles also figured amongst the Civil Servants, as might be expected for those in administrative functions, but Shapers and Resource Investigators were under-represented.

When it comes to promotion, the ability to play an effective part in a team is among the factors taken into consideration for the higher ranking jobs. Once in these jobs Civil Servants are able to control the size of teams in which they operate without external constraint. All in all Civil Servants have a starting advantage when it comes to forming effective policy-making groups.

The paradox, then, is that politicians and senior public servants are in many respects better fitted for the critical aspects of each other's ostensible duties. Senior public servants have the time, inclination, and natural ability to formulate new policies. Politicians, on the other hand, have the drive, energy, and the persuasive skill to turn policies into acceptable forms of action.

Exchange of roles

It is true, of course, that a certain amount of exchanging of roles goes on once politicians enter office. The formal and informal systems diverge under pressures that are created. Those in political life attend so many functions that they are obliged to leave some policy considerations to officials, while still retaining the outward appearance of being in charge.

CASE STUDY – DISTRIBUTION OF ROLES BETWEEN CIVIL SERVANTS AND POLITICIANS

Some insight into the nature of the relationship between Civil Servants and politicians was afforded us over the years using Cambridge as a vantage point. This opportunity came about partly because of our close link with two Ministries, but partly also because Cambridge was used as a major conference centre at which Government Ministers often made widely quoted policy statements at the conferences they address.

A recurring observation is that it is rare for a Government Minister to write his speeches except where he is addressing his own political supporters. This we witnessed at a Cambridge conference. A Minister was accompanied by three faceless officials, none of whom overtly seemed to play any part in the proceedings. This trio was taken aback by the unexpectedly bold question: 'Which of you wrote the speech?' The answer came in one raised hand, a delighted smile, and the counter-question: 'Did you like it?' The speech-writer turned out to be the most junior member of the travelling hierarchy with the other two members being the writer's immediate superior and the Minister's personal assistant.

The strength of hand of those within public administration is indicated by the fact that some Ministers never meet the individuals who write their speeches. In these cases the shadow writer will occupy a more humble position than one who is close to the Minister: yet while he languishes in obscurity, he enjoys in effect remarkable power and influence. An account from a well-informed source of the origins of one of the most important pieces of post-war industrial legislation illustrates the route by which new policies can see the light of day.

CASE STUDY – A FORTUNATE MISTAKE

One day a young Oxford graduate was given the task of writing a speech for a Minister who was to address an industrial conference. This imaginative young man in his innocence drew on a number of ideas of his own that had not even been discussed with his superiors. He elaborated on these ideas in commendable but unsupervised prose while his boss was away on holiday. The text was typed and duly placed on the Minister's desk. When the shadow writer's superior realized how far the junior had overstepped the mark, he attempted to get the speech withdrawn for revision. 'No, I like it,' the Minister told him. So the speech was given as it stood.

The salient point was picked up by *The Times*. Journalists speculated. The Minister defended 'his' position while treating the matter as being 'under consideration'. In due course there was a change of Ministers but the matter was now firmly established on the agenda of the Ministry and in due course a bill was introduced and became law.

Policies that originate with officials carry the advantage that they will certainly be vetted by Ministers and accepted, modified or rejected. There are possibilities here of building up an effective working relationship, with the twin arms of government recognizing the part that each can best play. The story about the young Oxford graduate however does not illustrate typical practice but was told to me by an official precisely because it represents an aberration of the system. Government is not supposed to work like that.

Imbalance in government

A Team Role approach to government could involve both its professional and political arms. It would encompass the generation of ideas; the assessment of them; and decision-making. The last of these three processes is peculiar to elected representatives. Balance can be achieved only if the other two processes precede the third and have a fair degree of independence. Constitutional orthodoxy, based on total political control over government, can stop this from occurring as it should. It is susceptible to producing a systems imbalance since there is no checking mechanism. This danger is especially liable to occur in the many instances when plans are conceived at the political level without the support of a professional management team to formulate the project and assess its feasibility.

CASE STUDY – TRIUMPH COUPLED WITH DISASTER

At the original time of writing this chapter the publication of Peter Hall's *Great Planning Disasters*, with case studies from the United States, Britain and Australia, brought out the massive consequences of intrepid initiatives by politicians acting alone or in concert. An example is the Anglo-French Concorde, described by Hall as 'perhaps the costliest commercial blunder in history', though for sheer rate of cost escalation it scarcely rivals the Sydney Opera House.

Concorde began as a report on supersonic transport by a committee entirely composed of air interests. The report in itself scarcely constituted a project and was never even made public. Yet the Minister responsible acted boldly as he explained with disarming frankness to a House of Commons Expenditure Committee:

> *'It was quite clear to me that were I as Minister to go to the Treasury the money would not be forthcoming. So in June, 1959, I went to France and I took advantage of the then Paris Air Show to suggest to the French that they should co-operate with the British in developing Concorde. It was in this way that I started. In retrospect I have to admit that my Department and I had no knowledge at all and had made no attempt at all to estimate the size of the potential market.'*

The need to find a new aircraft to keep the ailing British aircraft industry busy, after a history of cancelled aircraft; the importance of the aircraft workers' vote (after a change of government, a new Minister had been appointed who was also the parliamentary representative of the constituency where Concorde was being built); and the belief (mistaken, as it happened) once the dire facts of the project began to emerge, that continuation with Concorde was the price that Britain had to pay to appease Charles de Gaulle (the belief based on his opposition to Britain's entry to the European Common Market) were all factors that kept Concorde alive.

Many projects and programmes that are entirely political in origin have an unhappy ending. It is not uncommon for them to result in effects which are the exact opposite of what was intended. Measures to protect tenants or indigenous industries, for example, have all too often increased their ultimate plight.

It is not that political sincerity or the will to help is lacking. Political reverses have much to do with the failure to forecast how isolated measures will affect the system as a whole. Electorally attractive but oversimple solutions to problems may founder on the hard bedrock of reality.

Yet the real crisis in government has less to do with adversity in itself than with what ensues from setbacks. It is in the nature of things that politicians never have fallback programmes. To proclaim an open change of line would be to risk the disaffection of supporters and to prepare a path into the political wilderness. What therefore happens is that political dictation of policy gives way to a sudden loss in political control and direction. Power and responsibility begin to seep back, as inconspicuously as possible, into the hands of permanent officials. These, being more *au fait* with the affairs of state, less subject to day-to-day pressures, and enjoying long term rather than transient appointments, are well placed to come up with their own saving line. This is not the way government is intended to operate. Nor has such a sequence much to commend it from the point of view of efficiency.

The reasons why politicians are so difficult to weld together into efficient teams have been discussed earlier. Yet there is one exception to the rule that does not conflict with what has been learned about successful teams during our studies. This exception centres on the principle of a team supporting a single but elected figure.

Presidential government

The merit of a presidential style of government is that whoever is successful is able to create his or her own team. The ideal arrangement leaves the presidential figure free to go outside the ranks of colleagues (and possible rivals) and to select those with whom it is possible to establish a close and effective working relationship.

The American system of Presidential primaries offers a particularly interesting example of how two basically conflicting systems can be combined to this end. Candidates and their teams are presented to the electorate for their initial choice. This is a prelude to the choice between two successful candidates that occurs later in the Presidential election. A single powerful figure with an effective back-up team can take full advantage of opportunities but equally can succumb to the most dangerous risks. Some of the teams formed on this pattern in our experiments were amongst the most successful but others of them were conspicuous amongst those producing the worst results.

The Presidential primary system offers an extra sifting of candidates that allows the electorate more choice in selecting an ultimately powerful figure and team, improves the likelihood of a favourable outcome and is therefore a brilliant assay at a difficult problem. If, however, we were to apply the principles of team design to the management of public affairs, the Presidential system and its local equivalents are not to be recommended with confidence. Instead, we would prefer the balanced team of the type that has triumphed so well in our experiments. In that team it is not the Chairman (or the President) who is the dominant figure. The Chairman, particularly when that person happens to be a Co-ordinator, is no more than a people-manager who draws on the resources of a talented group. The focus shifts across from the cult of a personality with the associated aides to the potential of the team as a whole.

Team role interaction

Accordingly, our preferred suggestion for the better management of public affairs is for a change in role relationships within government. To this end, its political arm should primarily concern itself with final decision-making, with supervision of its Ministries, and with enhancing its special responsibilities for close contact and communication with the public. In so doing, it should disengage from the demanding task of developing detailed plans to meet major problems.

The intricate and often slow operation of planning is better handled by those who are able to control the group size of their own teams; who can heed individual performance assessed in previous tasks; who can take account of Team Role balance; and who can ensure that members have the qualities that match the Team Role for which they are envisaged. In other words, the permanent employees of government meet this specification better than the elected political representatives themselves. If this is so, there is much to be said for readjusting the relative responsibilities of elected representatives and government officials. Each group needs to be deployed in a way that is most fitted to the service it can render.

We might then reach this conclusion: democracy is likely to run into operating difficulties. This is certainly the case where the intent is that the maximum number of people participates in the decision-making process and equally where that authority is transferred to overworked elected representatives who are expected to assume the total responsibilities of government. Government, in practice, depends on both elected representatives and career officials. It is only through building up a pattern of interlocking accountability, widely recognized and accepted, that democratic government can function efficiently.

Public servants are not expected to produce plans and options in their own right, for they are regarded as being primarily there to enact decisions that are already made. Yet the lessons of industry teach us that new developments seldom succeed unless those responsible for their execution also have an active part to play in planning what is to be done. It is far better that this role is overt rather than surreptitious. And if it is overt, the political arm of government must change to allow it to focus more on the management of the civil servants. Politicians might then do better to concentrate on priorities and decisions; and civil servants, on policies and plans.

Better government is essentially about how different groups of people with different terms of reference can work within a common structure. And within that structure it is about how teams are best formed to make each group more effective. Any society that develops such an arrangement, that learns as part of that process how to construct the right teams of people, of whom to ask the right questions, and how to take advantage of the answers is well set up to promote its own well-being.

Summary

- In politics, the problems of balance are often multiplied by the propensity of all politicians to be of certain roles, and all Civil Servants to be of others.

- Ironically, most Civil Servants are ideally suited to making decisions judiciously, whereas politicians are generally more suited to driving decisions through.

- The Presidential style of government offers more opportunity to put a team together well, but relies on the leading figure having a good understanding of teams.

Chapter 13

Thirty years later

The events described in this book, together with those that followed its publication, have spanned an unusually long period of time. The experiments at Henley began in the late 1960s and continued until shortly before the appearance of the first edition of *Management Teams* in 1981. No less remarkable than the length of this research period was the fact that the book reached its peak sales 9 years after first publication and has never been out of print since.

The theory of Team Roles took a long time to emerge, amid all the many variables that combine to mask the detection of key factors. But once the theory had been shown to rest on sound foundations, useful applications quickly followed. A renewed focus on improving the balance of teams created a momentum of its own. Another significant consequence was the level of interest on the part of individuals. Many were keen to learn more about their own Team Role profiles and to discover how and where they could take most advantage of their potential.

The problem in writing *Management Teams* had been to know where to draw the line in terms of the presentation of a large amount of material. After consultation with the publisher, we decided to present the conduct and outcome of the research in narrative form. Inevitably, this approach to the presentation of material did not satisfy everyone. Some people needed more convincing, as I later discovered when conducting a weekend workshop for international lawyers. Without specific evidence, they would not accept any verdict or conclusions that might be offered! And so I have recovered the details from the 2 experimental years when we had made forecasts, addressed in sealed envelopes to the secretary of the exercise, on the predicted outcome and presented them in a way that met the need. These figures have since been displayed many times, but as they did not appear in print in the original book, they are included here.

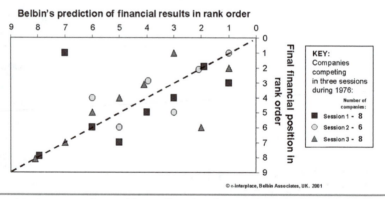

Figure 13.1   Teams formed by Belbin for the Henley Business Game.

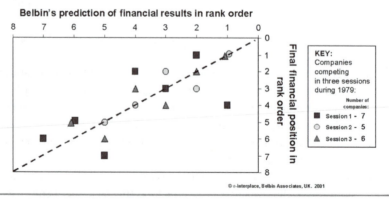

Figure 13.2   Teams formed by the Directorate for the Henley Business Game.

The case for predictive validity

Forecasts supported by outcomes are technically referred to as 'predictive validity'. To my mind this is the most stringent of tests. Instead, I find that people tend to ask about the 'reliability' of results, a subject on which test constructors tend to focus. I think this has led to a great deal of confusion. In colloquial terms 'reliability' implies: 'can one rely on what is claimed?' Technically, 'reliability' carries another meaning, being a statistical term, which in effect relates to 'consistency'. For example, the upholders of 'reliability' contend that items on a single scale in psychometric tests should be consistent with other items in measuring the same thing.

Consistency may have no bearing on validity. Being consistently wrong in making a forecast is no virtue. Some test constructors have made items in tests so consistent with one another that they become repetitive and tedious and predict nothing. In relation to Team Roles we knew that their composition depended on clusters of similar but different items. With the right combination they would produce an effective contribution to team performance. That concept governed the strategy of our research.

After the experiments at Henley ended, the methods and ideas we had formulated were put to use. They found immediate application in management teams, project teams, research and development teams, and product development teams. These experiences in the field generated lessons in learning. The first lesson concerned presentation: two of the terms we had been using had to be changed to make them more acceptable. The occasional managing director attending an educational workshop was not too pleased to be defined as a 'Company Worker'. Nor was it politically correct to refer to a gifted but young and low-ranking individual as a 'Chairman'. There were fewer red faces once the former term was transformed into 'Implementer' (IMP) and the latter into 'Co-ordinator' (CO).

The specialist role

In the original Henley experiments all the participants were equal at the same starting line: no one had the advantage of prior knowledge. This condition made it easier to identify the particular roles and contributions that given individuals were predisposed to take. But for the purpose of assessing the effectiveness of teams it was an artificial situation. People are seldom equal at the starting blocks for expert knowledge will afford some teams a head start. That much we learned when we started to advise real teams in the industrial world. 'Never reinvent the wheel' is a favoured adage. So managers putting together teams to tackle real challenges would first seek to find an 'expert' in a key area of knowledge and experience. There could be no presumption that such an expert would bear any distinct Team Role profile. And so it proved. Yet continuing research uncovered several revealing facts about typical 'experts'. The first was that many did not care for teamwork. They were not keen to join teams. But on the other hand they did like to be consulted and to share their knowledge with others. In practice, rather than inviting them into a team, a more effective approach to drawing on their knowledge was for a key person to engage them in interpersonal consultation *before* a team meeting was set up. The alternative was to demand their attendance at a team meeting. Then if they did contribute they would deliver their expertise with enthusiasm, failing to notice that their inputs were not being either listened to or understood. A number of 'experts' agreed to take our battery of psychometric tests. While they varied considerably in terms of personality, there were two features that stood out. The first was that they tended to have superior scores on a measure of mental ability (the CTA). The second was that on the PPQ (a measure on constructs), their construct range was on the low side. From this a picture emerged of individuals who were clever but narrow. That might explain their lack of interest in the matters being discussed within the team when they fell outside the 'expert's' areas of competence. Perhaps that is the price paid for excessive specialism.

If experts are to be enrolled in a team, or consulted beforehand, it became important to measure these typical tendencies. In place of psychometric tests we had now developed a new way of measuring team roles based on a Self-Perception Inventory (the SPI). This covered all eight Team Roles that we had identified in the Henley experiments and we now added a ninth – the Specialist (SP) role. One can argue that this is not really Team Role but rather a functional role being centred not on behaviour but on preferring to engage in a particular duty in line with acquired knowledge and experience.

However, the counter argument is that true SPs may not have any specialism when starting off in a team, but possess a desire to become an expert in an ever-narrowing field. They behave in a way that fails to accord with existing Team Roles but instead reveals their SP potential. The value of this concept is to place latent SPs in jobs that offer scope for developing their preferred work-tendency. This carries the additional advantage that expertise can be fostered from within the organisation.

Beyond psychometrics

The problem now was to detect individuals who possessed the potential to act as SPs and to filter out those with technical backgrounds who did not behave as effective SPs might. Here psychometric tests could offer us little help. But we had in any case reached the point where we could no longer carry on with the same diagnostic tools that we had used at Henley in our experimental work. These tools are so demanding in professional time as to preclude their everyday use in industry. In substitution we had developed the SPI containing nine measures, eight dealing with the identified Team Roles and the ninth a measure built to identify the SP tendency. As a control a tenth scale was introduced containing attractive items that carried no Team Role significance. The advantage of the SPI was that scores could be computerised and eventually inputted and downloaded online.

One limitation of psychometric tests is that they rely on self-reporting. There is a presumption that individuals fully understand themselves. This can be far from the case. A failure in self-perception was a common feature of some of the problem people we encountered in industry. They would see themselves as strong in areas that others considered a weakness. By acting on this notion and illusion they would create difficulties both for themselves and others. Information about how individuals are perceived by others is no less important than information about how individuals perceive themselves. With this in mind we developed Observer Assessments containing adjectives and adjectival phrases that described behaviour that was typical of each Team Roles. All the observer needed to do was to tick the words that applied to the person. There were two lists of words. One contained the strengths associated with each Team Role and the other the 'allowable weakness' that often accompanied the strength. Information from the SPI and from Observer Assessments could be fed into a new computer system called *Interplace*. The optimal reconciliation was calculated and the inputs were then transformed into a report available to be downloaded by licensed users anywhere in the world.

Common misconceptions

Although the language of Team Roles is now taught in universities and business schools all over the world, there are nevertheless still some residual misconceptions. I address some of these now.

Misconception	Reality
Team Roles are measures of personality	Teams roles are functions of the different demands made on team members if the team is to become effective. Individuals respond to these demands in different ways.

(*Continued*)

Misconception	Reality
People cannot change their Team Roles	While individuals will have a certain affinity for certain Team Roles and less for others, in all cases learning plays a part. Hence some degree of adjustment is always possible.
Team Roles vary with culture	The same basic types of Team Roles contribution have been identified in all cultures. But the manner of their expression depends on social customs.
People in some types of society cannot adapt to Team Roles	The structure of authority sometimes makes it impossible for Team Roles to flourish. But once tyranny is removed, new personal growth possibilities arise.
People should be encouraged to overcome their weaknesses to allow them to perform well in each of the Team Roles	Strong performance in one Team Role makes it quite likely there will be a weaker performance in another. It is more important to perform certain Team Roles well than to cover the whole range where the effects would be to deny Team Role opportunity to others.

Case studies in using Belbin

Introduction

To illustrate the application of Team Role theory I have collected a cross section of 11 case studies. Their nature, country of origin and the organisation are set out below.

1	Changing a company's style	Norway	Linjegods AS
2	Helping to bridge the culture gap	Czech Republic	Coneo
3	Use of team roles in change strategy	UK and Germany	Social Innovation and Allied Domecq
4	Using Interplace® in a school	UK	Richmond School
5	An expedition to Morocco	UK	Take Footsteps Ltd
6	Linking the work of teams	Denmark	H. Lundbeck
7	Creating productive working relationships	UK	Leading Edge Performance Development Ltd
8	Development of an R & D team	UK	SBS Integrate Ltd
9	Developing 'teaming' as a working model	South Africa	7i Management Consultants
10	Developing team roles in a range of organisations	UK	Worsley Associates Ltd
11	The story of a personal transformation	UK	CERT Consultancy & Training

1 Changing a company's style

Asbjorn Aanesen (Organisational Manager)

Linjegods AS, Norway

Linjegods AS was founded in 1972 and is Norway's leading supplier of logistics and transport services. The company has a turnover in excess of £2 billion Norwegian Kronor and reported a profit of 78 million in 2001. Linjegods has 1160 employees and is made up of five regions, with each being an independent profit centre headed by a regional manager and a management team. The CEO's management team comprises the regional managers as well as six technical managers.

The company was in contact with Meredith Belbin as far back as the 1980s with a view to find a suitable tool for team-building. Later in the 1990s, team-building, following the Belbin method, was introduced in order to create and develop regional management teams as well as the company's senior management team.

Linjegods has benefited greatly from the system and our experience can be briefly summarized as follows.

Management stability

An analysis of the company's structure and management revealed an unusually high turnover of senior managers in the 1970s and 1980s. Senior managers and their management teams were constantly leaving, to the benefit of competitors who promptly took over customers and market shares. It therefore became necessary, early in the 1990s, to focus on the importance of the stability of the management of the company. The Belbin approach became the key to achieve this stability by creating an understanding of the whole, and of the relationship between professional roles, Team Roles, work roles, and political roles.* The process involved developing productive teams and extracting the best from each member and from the group as a whole. To achieve this goal, group members were encouraged to trust one another, to believe that fellow members deserved success and to value diversity. We have been successful in meeting all these aims.

---

* The allusion to work roles and political roles relates to material contained in *Beyond the Team* (Butterworth-Heinemann, 2000).

Management diversity

A further traditional feature of the management recruitment practice of the company was the 'beckoning' principle – management invited in those whom they liked. Many members of our management teams proved to be suspiciously similar, as was revealed with the aid of the Belbin team measures. The first time these measures were applied to the company's senior management they revealed a surprising number of Shapers, a number of Specialists, and a total absence of Team Workers. The teams were uniform and demanding but proved unable to 'grow' by adding to their attributes or utilizing resources. During the 1990s attention was therefore focused on the need to diversify the teams. Here Belbin's methods played a significant role in revealing the presence or absence of certain attributes and increasing team members' awareness of each other. In a restart operation, teams that previously had lacked diversity were broadened with the aid of a combination of development and recruitment/shedding of managers. This change has, without exception, resulted in better teams and better management.

Management development

Information about the internal workings of the teams has provided the individual manager with increased self-awareness of his/her behaviour and suitability for the job. Against this background participants have been given the opportunity to assess their own roles and implications for their careers. Feedback from fellow team members has shown whether 'the map matches the territory' for the individual manager. In my assessment, Belbin's unique method is particularly well suited to personal development and training measures because the approach is 'open and balanced' in a way that other methods are not. By this I mean that the method is balanced in its descriptive form and free of extreme formulations which might otherwise have blocked all discussion and put participants on the defensive in relation to other participants. Experience has shown that the interest of the participants increases sharply as the process progresses. The result is a greater willingness to participate in subsequent development programmes and a higher level of motivation. In these programmes the team and the individual participants have received suggestions for work sharing and the development of roles and needed personal skills. Improved evaluation has led to faster progress in taking corrective measures.

2 Helping to bridge the culture gap

Jana Krajcarova (Consultant)

Coneo, Czech Republic

Coneo is a Czech consulting and educational company which has been working with the Interplace® system since 1998. Two years have been spent in transferring the system into the Czech environment and its application has been verified in the case of 800 candidates.

I would like to share our experience in the individual use of a test series for the top management at Schneider. Schneider is a French company that owns a production plant in the Czech Republic. The plant is a former state-owned company that Schneider had bought and modernized. Later the original staff started to work in a completely new-built plant. One problem facing Schneider was how to change the employees' way of thinking. A French person, a top manager who didn't hesitate, among other things, to learn good Czech, was appointed to the position of executive director. He found that he had to face problems caused by the different culture and mentality of the Czech employees.

Our consulting company – Coneo – was engaged to weld together the top management team, consisting of both French and Czech managers. We used Belbin tests and special team-building training methods. Everything looked very promising, except for the area of quality control. It seemed that here a special approach was called for. The French executive director asked us to carry out individual coaching of a particular (Czech) quality control manager whose performance was not satisfactory.

After the situation analysis we found the quality control manager to be an outstanding and hard-working professional. Despite this finding, the executive manager let us know that he was considering dismissing the quality control manager but wanted to offer a last chance before doing so.

What was the cause of the problem?

We set out to look at the tasks and aims of the job and to verify the desired outcomes. This brought us to a very interesting conclusion. The key problem was the actual specification of the quality control manager position and the different views on its operation. We set about trying to find out which specific and objective tool could be used to allow both managers to find common ground and to use their strongest points. A logical and very successful solution was to use the Belbin Interplace® complete series and to use it for both managers and for the position of quality control manager.

Of course we started with the explanation of our intention and with 'selling the idea'. Then we went on with SPI tests for both managers and there we came across a bit of a hindrance: the French manager didn't have sufficient language feeling for Czech and English to be able to undergo the tests in either of these languages. Therefore we used the French version of the tests, worked out the key and, of course, inserted the results into the Czech version of the Interplace® system. Also, when the observers were evaluating both candidates, the rest of the top management team members were given the opportunity to work with French words if desired.

After processing and evaluating both profiles the first source of communication problems became obvious: the executive manager was, in his profile, unambiguously a strong Shaper, while the quality control manager was, unambiguously again, an extreme Monitor Evaluator.

In specifying the position of quality control manager it became clear that the executive director was seeking a managing type of Shaper, a Co-ordinator, and an Innovator, one who should manage the quality as a whole, while, in reality, the existing manager paid too much attention to details.

It was a fantastic advantage to use all the outputs and diagrams to clarify the nature of the problem. The quality control manager stopped taking the reservations of his superior personally and managed to take things more easily, which can be very important in the case of someone with a strong Monitor Evaluator profile. The executive manager, on the other hand, started to understand the strong points in his subordinate. The real cause of all the problems lay in setting the aims and deciding on the control. Our first move was to pull down the personal barriers. This was made easier thanks to the fact that *both* the subordinate and his superior had been 'tested'.

In the second phase we started to deal with the specification of the quality control manager position. With the aim of retaining this professionally capable employee, the new specification of this position was set out and its responsibilities were also distributed to other members of the top management. In other words, the unsuccessful effort of 'adjusting' the employee to the given position was turned into the more successful exercise of customizing the position for a capable employee.

Of course this approach had a limited application because other objectives had to be met and needed attention. One of the desired outputs for the quality control manager was a personal development plan. Here the aim was to help him communicate better with other Team Roles of his colleagues and so enable him to better develop the system of leadership in the area of quality control.

I would like to point out that we managed to solve this sensitive problem not only without any personal frustrations and animosity, but also with a significant increase in the motivation of both managers. It also must be said that a year after testing, as a part of the evaluation process, both managers claimed to have become friends!

3 Use of team roles in change strategy

Paul Wielgus, Chris Zanetti

Social Innovation, UK Allied Domecq, Germany

Allied Domecq Spirits and Wines is the second largest drinks company in the world, with a turnover in excess of £3 billion, and employs over 10,000 people internationally.

In 1994 Allied created a unique internal and growth consultancy, ADventure. The mission was to create a culture of innovation throughout the company, and liberate the social capital potential latent in the diverse teams around the business. A key tool in this process was Belbin Interplace®, which was used extensively.

Between 1998 and 2001, head of ADventure (AD), Paul Wielgus, worked closely with the Managing Director of Allied in Central and Eastern Europe (CEE), Chris Zanetti. Their mission was to harness the cultural diversity across 12 countries, in order to achieve stretching corporate goals.

Prior to 1998, the culture in the region was very directive, run on a command and control basis from a regional HQ in Brussels. The markets were dependent on orders issued from the 'centre'. There was little or no networking below the level of MDs and little transfer of best practice.

However, there was a strong 'work ethic' and some excellent work in connecting with consumers. It was evident, however, that the company was not using its resources of people, systems, and creativity in the most effective way for the benefit of consumers and ultimately AD as a whole. The company simply had previously not recognized the potential in the diversity of the people in the region.

Changing the culture

As newly appointed MD, Chris called in Paul to help with his new strategy for CEE. Chris wanted to transform the culture completely as follows:

- He wanted to create a culture of interdependence across the region.
- He wanted to understand, identify, and harness the skills of the people and teams within and across the region, in order to harness the potential and deliver the strategy and business goals. The Belbin instrument was a fundamental tool to achieve this.

The initial focus in implementing the strategy was on leadership and team-building and creating the capability to deliver the strategy. Specifically, Belbin was used to:

■ Develop organisational trust comprising trust in each other and trust in the team to deliver.

■ Give a common language across the region, and prepare the foundation for a powerful network that could be relied on for information and support.

■ Help identify specific talents and roles for individuals across the region, and facilitate the allocation of Team Roles to specific projects.

■ Enable the company to develop a culture of interactivity that was no longer top-down, but sought input at all levels in order to achieve company goals effectively.

■ Build energy during the many workshops that were run during the period, through using Belbin as a component part of a range of innovative 'action learning' interventions.

The outcomes

■ The creation and delivery of a credible and robust strategy, which delivered 55% profit growth in less than 3 years.

■ The development of a rich, diverse team culture, which developed its skills in the delivery of high-quality service and brands in the consumer marketing arena.

■ Powerful personal and professional development for individuals.

■ A strong reputation for customer of choice within and outside of Allied Domecq. In particular, the region posted some impressive results in their Employee Opinion Survey, particularly around dimensions such as team-working, job satisfaction, customer service, and learning.

4 Using Interplace® in a school

Delphine Rushton
Richmond School, UK

Richmond School, North Yorkshire, is a rural comprehensive school with 1600 students in the 11–18 age range and 145 teaching and support staff. The inspection report by the Office for Standards in Education (Ofsted) described it as 'a very good school with some outstanding features'. Exam results at both GCSE and post-16 are well above the national average.

The school has a strong tradition of continuous improvement and staff development and to this end, invested in Belbin Interplace® in 1998. This was quite unusual because, although widely used in the business environment and higher education, Belbin Interplace® is less used within the British compulsory education sector. Yet it has much to offer. Long gone are the days when a teacher dwelt solely within the classroom and subject specialism. Education is now a complex, dynamic, and pressurized environment. Working to a demanding agenda of government reforms, and technological, pedagogical, and social change, teachers and support staff depend on each other more than ever before. A complex range of skills, qualities, and experiences is needed. At Richmond, like many other schools, there is a matrix management structure and it is common for one teacher to be a member of three different teams. Staff need to be in the right position in order to maximize their potential, maintain job satisfaction, and work in a complementary way with colleagues. In this context, Belbin Interplace® has become integrated into human resource practices in three ways.

Recruitment

Belbin Interplace® is used in recruitment, providing an individual profile that complements other traditional processes such as the interview, presentation, and model lesson. Two examples make the point. The Administration Department has burgeoned in recent years to meet increasing demands for sophisticated support services. Belbin Interplace® has been used in recruitment in order to ensure that new members complement the team and have the attributes most suited to work efficiently and calmly to tight deadlines and managing a range of people, including fellow staff, students, and the public. Similarly, in 2002, the governing body appointed a new head teacher. Belbin Interplace® was used as part of the rigorous three-day process and provided information to help the Governors appoint the person most suited to the strategic needs of the school.

Individual career development

Career progression is an important part of staff development and retention and there are many possible routes: Head of Department; Pastoral Leader; Cross-curricular Co-ordinator such as ICT or Careers; and Senior Manager. Here, Belbin Interplace® is used for individual career development as part of mentoring provision. Whether it be a young teacher considering his/her first move from classroom operator into a managerial post, or a senior manager wishing to pursue further leadership roles, it provides feedback on team strengths and career direction. Unconnected with assessment of performance linked with pay, it helps staff evaluate their current responsibilities and contributions. Staff have not had access to this kind of feedback before and they have found it to be both illuminating and productive.

Team-building

For the experienced managers and their teams, Belbin provides a language with which to understand, engage, and develop different team members. This is especially so where much-needed talents lie hidden or under-used. It has been used by the Senior Management Team to review team characteristics and consequent influences on decision-making. It has also been used in a counselling capacity to foster positive interpersonal communications.

The school's 'business success' is measured not only quantitatively in exam results, but also qualitatively in the richness of school life and the deep-seated learning experiences which students will draw on throughout their lives. Both kinds of success are made or marred by the impact of teachers. The effective deployment and development of staff increase the likelihood of students, in turn, receiving a good start to life. Discreetly, Belbin Interplace$^{®}$ has made a valuable contribution in this way.

A further indication of the school's appreciation of the Belbin method is perhaps seen in the fact that it has recently invested in 'GetSet'* so that students themselves can benefit from the Belbin Team Role theory as they make their own career and further education choices.

5   An expedition to Morocco

Ric Broad (Executive Director)
Take Footsteps Ltd, UK

The background

Ric Broad was a captain in the Army Physical Training Corps. As soon as he retired from the Army, he set about using his acquired skills to help in the development of young people. He has submitted the following case study.

---

* GetSet is a programme offering personalized advice, akin to that offered by Interplace$^{®}$, but has been devised for those without work experience.

Expeditions abroad

Since picking up and reading *Team Roles at Work* 10 years ago, and gaining accreditation in the use of Interplace® and Team Roles 4 years later, I have been busy applying the knowledge found therein (together with other gems from subsequent RMB books, such as *Beyond the Team*). The outcomes from the learning have provided recipients with a new sense of direction and myself with wanting to know more about Belbin Team Roles and other related material. I believe they can be applied to everyone.

Case study

Under my charge in an expedition to Morocco were Jim, Frank, Peter, John, Bill, Geoff, Kate, and Sophie. All were in danger of being *excluded* or *excluding themselves* from the educational establishment that they were currently attending. They were aged between 16 and 17 years and came from schools in the North East of England. At the start of a programme designed to help these young people develop essential life skills, they were introduced to Belbin Team Roles. On a one-to-one basis, they were assisted in completing the Belbin Self-Perception Inventory (SPI). At the end of the programme, Observer Assessments would be added to confirm the profile of the student.

The situation

The *status quo* was one of not feeling valued, lack of self-esteem and a general lack of trust in adults. Many of the young people would state: 'I am not good at anything' and then go on to explain about the problems at home and in the area that they were living in.

The beauty of using the outdoors in applying Belbin Team Roles for young people is that most young people enjoy being outdoors and they tend to act more naturally away from the constraints of the educational establishment.

Once the SPIs were printed out, each student could see quite clearly their main strengths, as they perceived themselves. However the main point is this:

- The computer could not distinguish if the student was from a high fee-paying private school or a state comprehensive school (I accept that there are excellent, good, and not so good in both!) and provided data without any prejudice.
- At last some light showed at the end of the tunnel. The students were able to recognize that they had talent and were able to start to contribute to the wider

Belbin Associates

3-4 Bennell Court

West Street

Comberton

Cambridge

CB23 7EN

As outlined in the author's note, the Self-Perception Inventory (SPI) and scoring sheet found in this new edition of *Management Teams* is now nearly thirty years old and has been superseded by a fully normed and computerized version that includes the ninth role of Specialist.

To try this new version, we would be delighted to send you one free on-line version, which nomally costs £25 inclusive of VAT.

To register for this free on-line SPI, please send this card to the address overleaf.

(We can only accept the original card. Photocopies will not be accepted. We will only accept one per email address. Belbin Associates also have the right to refuse if they consider multiple applications are being made.)

If you are looking to 'Belbin' a team/group of people, please contact the office to discuss the most cost-effective method available to you. Email info@belbin.com or phone +44 (0)1223 264975

Please send me a free on-line Belbin SPI, My details are as follows:

Name: _____

Organization: _____

Email address: _____

Tel. number: _____

☐ Please retain my details on the Belbin database to remain informed about developments picture. They started to see that they could make changes in themselves and contribute rather than blaming and reacting in a negative way.

On a short expedition all the teams were able to build on their Team Roles. When the students filled in the SPI they were extremely forthright and honest in completing them. Most of them found their self-image compatible with how they were seen by others. Only a couple found discordance between these images. During the trip the Co-ordinator, Jim, who was respected by all of the team, was able to get the team together and hold useful meetings to plan the next phase of the trip and allocate different tasks to the team. Kate was given the role of medical assistant to the team adult leader as she was high on the Team Worker role and was able to empathize and show care and consideration to the other team members. Peter always wanted to talk to other people on the journey and find out about bus or train timetables and what was going on in the area we ended up in, a perfect slot for a Resource Investigator! The team was not a *perfect team* by any means, but in the short team available to us, much was learned and practised by the students about different types of team contribution.

I could go on about each individual and how they contributed on the outdoor exercise in Belbin Team Role terms. For most of you familiar with Team Roles the characteristics of each role need no further explanation. The leading question is how does one measure how successful and useful Belbin Team Roles were on our journey? For me, the answer is quite simple: one measures it by the body language of those who used it after each review session; and, when returning home, their confidence in that they *did* have something to offer prospective employers, not only in skills, but also in terms of how they could fit in to a team.

Summary

Using Belbin Team Roles did not put the students 'into boxes', but provided another perspective in which they could view and gain feedback on their contribution in life. The students' current situation (2 years on) is that four have moved on to the world of work. One has gained employment as an assistant manager in a local business, one joined the armed services, two are at colleges of further education, and one unfortunately, due to lack of good local facilitation, made little headway and is not employed. I am convinced that using Belbin Team Roles provided us with an unseen structure for mounting the expedition and contributed in helping to shape the students' future. One thing is for sure, do not expect quick fixes, have faith, and keep up to date, for all the Belbin products are developing and improving with client–user feedback. It is a product for life and an adventure journey in its own right.

6 Linking the work of teams

Merete Hartwig Petersen (HRD Consultant)

H. Lundbeck, Denmark

About H. Lundbeck

H. Lundbeck is an international pharmaceutical company focused solely on agents acting on the central nervous system. H. Lundbeck's vision is to become the world leader in its focus areas of psychiatry and neurology with a mission to improve the quality of life for those suffering from psychiatric and neurological disorders. Cipramil/Cipralex is an anti-depression drug and it is Lundbeck's dominant product. About 5000 people are working at H. Lundbeck.

H. Lundbeck was established in 1915. In the 1930s the company moved into production and in the 1940s it moved into research.

Belbin's Team Roles at H. Lundbeck management training

About 2 years ago the Human Resource Development (HRD) division at H. Lundbeck started to work with Belbin's Team Roles. The HRD division is responsible for part of the Lundbeck management training. The management training is based on Kenneth Blanchard's concept of situational leadership and building high-performing teams. Building a high-performing team requires an awareness of not only the professional roles of the team members, but also a strong focus on the different Team Roles of the team members. Therefore, the managers are introduced to Belbin's Team Roles as a tool for making a 'high-performing team' more effective. After having finished their management training, the managers have the opportunity to ask the HRD division to help them work with the Team Roles.

Belbin's Team Roles in the Production division

In Production at H. Lundbeck, a lot of people are working in self-managing teams, and an obvious need has been seen to employ Belbin's Team Roles. Instead of focusing only on their professional roles, the team members have become aware of the different strengths and allowable weaknesses of their Team Roles and very often this focus has improved communication and co-operation in the teams. They often come to the sudden realization that the team member who differs from the rest of the team members should not be cast as an 'outsider' but can be a valuable acquisition for the team. Now the jobs are not only distributed among the team members according to the professional roles, but to a considerable extent according to the Team Roles.

For example, a team – Team A – was told on one occasion that they had difficulties in co-operating with Team B. The two teams came from different divisions. Team A came from a division that supported the processes in Production and Team B came from Production. Team A thought that they had a lot to offer to Team B, but they felt that Team B couldn't see this. So they thought they banged their heads against a brick wall every time they tried to offer their services and co-operation to Team B. They felt that Team B thought they were trying to meddle in their business instead of seeing it as a helping hand.

Having worked effectively with Belbin's Team Roles, Team A knew that one of the team members was a great Resource Investigator and Team Worker. So they decided that he should be the contact person for dealing with Team B. After this decision was made, the level of co-operation between the two teams greatly improved. The key to this improvement lay in emphasizing the advantages of co-operation between the two teams (with a view to creating a trustworthy relationship) instead of trying to persuade Team B of all the great qualities of Team A.

Belbin's Team Roles in the Research and Development division

In Research and Development (R & D), people do not work in teams to the same extent as they do in Production. Many specialists are employed in R & D in very particular fields and either fail to see the need or haven't had the opportunity of working in teams. The interesting question is whether they would become even better at doing their jobs – and so fulfilling H. Lundbeck's vision and mission – if they worked in teams and not only focused on their professional roles but also on their Team Roles. Some specialists see their profession as the main element in their work and take no account of the 'molecules' in their teammates.

Work in teams in R & D is now increasing. Scientists from R & D, brought together from across divisions, are discovering the benefits of combining and challenging each other's ideas in order to improve their work. The focus on Team Roles, and how they are distributed within the team, very often makes the work process much more fruitful, creative, and effective.

We have become aware that the advantages of working with Team Roles must be made very clear to those who are sceptical. In a scientific world like R & D, people are not familiar with the ideas springing from Human Resources. Therefore, it is critical to illustrate the 'hard core' advantages of focusing on the Team Roles. Unless this happens from the outset, one may not get a second chance.

7   Creating productive working relationships

Grant Davies

Leading Edge Performance Development Ltd, UK

Sheila Davidson and Alan Hardy worked in the Marketing and Sales division of a large utility company in North-West England. Sheila was the Head of Marketing and Sales and Alan was the Marketing Manager who reported to Sheila. They were experiencing some problems working together, and their working relationship had been deteriorating for some time.

Alan was an external appointment whom Sheila took on partly because he was seen as different, and not constrained by the organisational culture. He was an effective Marketing Manager with innovative ideas for marketing and good at networking and creating good relationships with clients and potential clients. He preferred to have a lot of autonomy in the way he operated, though at times he was seen by Sheila as a bit of a maverick and even occasionally as a 'loose cannon'.

One of Sheila's responsibilities was to present information about sales, progress, marketing results, etc. to her Director on a regular basis. Her Director was a man who required detail in every report. Sheila had no problem with this; she liked to provide detail and wanted the reports to 'be right'. She had a good relationship with her boss, which she wished to protect. The reports to him, however, were written by her two department managers as part of their regular responsibilities. Alan was one of the managers. Sheila felt that the reports she received from Alan were not detailed enough to be sent straight to her boss and so insisted on refining them herself before they were passed on. Alan was annoyed by this and saw Sheila as a 'control freak'.

The relationship had deteriorated to the point where Sheila was thinking that, despite his obvious talents, Alan must change or leave.

Belbin Team Role profiles obtained on both of them included the use of Observer Assessments. The Overall Assessment profiles are shown below.[*]

Overall Team Role profile for Sheila was:

CF ME SH PL SP IMP RI CO TW

Overall Team Role profile for Alan was:

SH PL RI CO ME SP TW CF IMP

Putting together the Team Role data and interview information, the following conclusions were drawn:

Strengths exhibited by Sheila

Completer–Finisher
Attention to detail. Very persistent when asking Alan for details during their meetings. Likes to get the reports 'right' (perfectionist).

Shaper
Tough – adamant that things should be done in a certain way.

Strengths exhibited by Alan

Shaper
Gets on with the job. Likes a fair degree of autonomy to use his own initiative.

Plant
Innovative, has different ideas, generates creative ways of marketing.

Resource Investigator
Likes to try new ideas, prefers overview to detail, good at networking.

Overplaying of strengths by Sheila

Completer Finisher
Overplaying attention to detail to the extent of being fussy. Frightened of failure – reflected by Alan's view of Sheila as a 'control freak'.

Reluctant to delegate – Alan feels she does not trust him to do the job properly, so she does it again herself.

---

[*] CF, Completer Finisher; CO, Co-ordinator; IMP, Implementer; ME, Monitor Evaluator; PL, Plant; RI, Resource Investigator; SH, Shaper; SP, Specialist; TW, Team Worker.

Overplaying of strengths by Alan

Resource Investigator

Easily bored – Alan is quickly turned off by detail and cannot see the point of it. Impulsive/erratic – Sheila sees Alan as unpredictable and a bit of a loose cannon.

Shaper

Impatient – Sees Sheila's attention to detail as an obstacle to getting on with the job.

Aggressive – Meetings with Sheila are often antagonistic.

Plant

Unorthodox – Likes to do things his way, which are very different from Sheila's ways.

How the situation was resolved

Here were two managers who both had a high preference for Shaper, so both had an inclination to be tough and dominant. However, their other preferred roles were very different; Sheila having a preference for Completer Finisher and Monitor Evaluator, and Alan for Plant and Resource Investigator.

To improve the relationship, Sheila needed to give greater recognition to Alan's PL and RI strengths and allow him to play to those. She could then acknowledge his achievements and he would feel valued. Instead she was asking him to play to his weaknesses in providing the kind of reports she required. Alan needed to recognize the strengths that Sheila could provide (CF and ME), that he did not have, which would enable them to be an effective management unit. Whilst an understanding of their Team Role preferences enabled them to do this, it did not solve the problem of the report writing.

When the Team Role profiles of Alan's team members were examined it was discovered that he had three people strong at Completer Finisher, with the necessary skills to provide the quality of report that Sheila was looking for. It was therefore agreed that *one* of these team members would be responsible for producing the detailed material of the report and would liaise directly with Sheila. Alan would focus on the overview that the report presented. Both seemed happy with this arrangement. Their relationship now improved dramatically. Overall, the exercise acted as an illustration of how fitting Team Role preferences for appropriate tasks can lead to improved team effectiveness and better working relationships.

8 Development of an R & D team

Solveig Bruce Stupples [*]

SBS Integrate Ltd, UK

Background to the problem

Active Biotech AB is a spinout from a large pharmaceutical company that now had to stand on its own feet. A new head of the R & D department had been appointed. He was a strong character, who created some turbulence in the organisation as he was trying to make the necessary changes. The organisational tradition was hierarchical and each manager was mainly concerned with defending his/her own territory without worrying about the whole organisation. The understanding of the business situation was minimal, since everyone had got his or her professional experience within a multinational company and was used to protection by other layers of management.

A new purpose

The new aim was to create an organisation built on team principles, where everyone in the management team felt involved in ownership and was prepared to be accountable for the total business. They also wanted to develop a team that was flexible enough to handle the rapid changes likely to happen within a company of this kind. They should also convey one common message down to the organisation and bridge the strategic perspective of the company down to an operational level.

According to the head of R & D, a process of 'remarkable transition' ensued:

- SBS Integrate Ltd was invited in, in September 2000, to help facilitate the team development process. The major tool that was introduced was M. Belbin's Team Roles at a 2-day workshop. Issues and interpersonal differences were highlighted and accepted by all.

- A follow-up workshop was held in January 2001.

- In June 2002, the team could conclude that the team goals had been reached and the team then set out new goals for the future.

---

[*] I first worked with Solveig in Sweden, where she proved a remarkably effective change agent in the Swedish pharmaceutical firm, Pharmacia, before she moved with her husband to the UK. R.M.B.

Result

Step 1: Workshop in September 2000

The Team Role profiling showed an intellectual group, relatively balanced with all Team Roles represented except for the Specialist. However, there were two Shapers, one of whom was the head of the team. He decided to step aside from the operational issues to allow the rest of the team to utilize their strengths better and develop team accountability. The head decided to utilize his other strengths (Plant in particular) to think of new ways to develop the business and the organisation.

Step 2: Follow-up workshop in January 2001

After a hesitant start and the first 'shock' of needing to take more responsibility, the team had started to develop and provided the material for identifying issues that needed to be addressed. Yet the team continued to behave much as before.

Step 3: Continued interaction between SBS Integrate and individual members of the team

This gave members the opportunity to develop themselves both within and outside the team framework.

Step 4: Achievements following the future goals workshop in June 2002

A remarkable transition has taken place, with the following consequences.

Focus

The team's agenda has moved from 'easy' items to discussing ways of increasing the effectiveness and efficiency of the organisation. The ability to lead and manage has improved dramatically.

The team

The team has changed since the beginning. Some people have left and others have entered, so allowing for the integration of the new members into a well-balanced team, clear in its purpose and goals, and committed to the highest levels of effectiveness and efficiency. Several members of the team have changed their work roles to bring them more into line with their strengths and Team Roles.

Measurable outcome

The organisation has become more business aware and flexible enough to adapt to ongoing changes. There is a greater readiness to utilize personal strengths and there is generally more interaction between team members. The most evident change has been in the conduct of successful research projects. That outcome accords with the general purpose of the company, for high performance in the R & D management team is a prerequisite for continued success.

9   Developing 'teaming' as a working model for the South African Revenue Services (SARS)

Carol Koffman, Natalie Robbs

7i Management Consultants, Sandton, South Africa

The South African Revenue Services (SARS) is currently undergoing a business process re-engineering (BPR) exercise, which began in 1999. The goal is to transform a government entity, characterized by a 'public service mindset', into a learning organisation capable of innovation and sustainability. The aim is to deliver services of the highest quality, at the lowest possible cost, and as speedily as possible. This switch has brought a focus on the five disciplines of a learning organisation, namely systematic thinking, building a shared vision, team learning, mental models, and personal mastery. In order to achieve the 'learning model' of working, SARS needed to challenge the validity of the previous hierarchical culture and its departmental structures.

The apparent challenge was twofold: first, the 'new' and 'transformed' work force profile had not been clearly articulated; and second, it was unclear how SARS would assess results if the current work force profile was not known in its entirety. In the 'new' democratic South Africa, organisations such as SARS are characterized by great diversity in the make-up of their staff complement in respect of competencies and suitability. SARS has handled this by looking at team leader roles and team member roles, each requiring a unique intervention, such as training, and taking into account their functional roles.

In July 2001, 7i Management Consultants was subcontracted to design a Team Leader Training Pre-Assessment Tool to determine the content, depth, level, and range of training to be delivered. 7i used the Belbin Team Role Inventory as a complement to the required roles already identified by SARS. The results of the Team Role profiles were then checked against a list of management-leadership competencies identified by the managers within SARS as essential for the re-engineering process to be successful and for the future business of SARS.

The overall conclusion from this process was that the very question of the team leadership role would have to be revisited and revised in the light of the new focus on vision, self-awareness, adaptability, and doing things in a new way.

7i then had the opportunity to examine team member roles and in May 2002, was awarded a tender to conduct a comprehensive skills audit, demographic profile overview, and competency profiling exercise within the Customs Business Division within SARS. Team member assessments, using the Belbin Team Role Inventory, were conducted with over 1600 team members in Customs. The purpose was to determine the content and type of training required for team members to ensure that the 'teaming' concept worked. The need to undergo the assessment was based on the following reasons:

■ An undue selection of the same sort of people (team leaders) for training;

■ Team members feeling overlooked and therefore demotivated, as a consequence;

■ Enthusiasm and eagerness to learn, despite feeling sidelined (a climate survey was included in the Belbin process); and

■ The failure to develop *all* team members was exacerbating the feeling of demoralization.

The team member assessments proved to be morale-boosting. Team-building exercises gave attention to, and recognition of, each team member. Information on Team Role profiles helped in interventions for the development of the team members and the team as a whole.

A very appealing feature of the Belbin Team Role Inventory (in terms of South Africa's National Qualifications Framework [NQF] criteria) is that the Inventory is based on experimental observations, not psychological constructs. Thus, a training programme that lends itself to seeing observable improvement in behaviour provides great advantages.

To summarize then, what makes Belbin preferable in a South African context is that it complies with the legislative requirements in the following particulars:

■ It assesses behaviour, not personality;

■ The gap between self-scoring and the observer scoring provides valid guidelines as to strengths and weakness in individual Team Roles;

■ All scoring and reporting is electronic, making the presentation and interpretation of results more reliable and making the generation of reports more efficient and comprehensive;

■ It has over 21 years of research, application, and improvement and enjoys widespread acceptance all over the world;

■ The reports have proved to be invaluable in identifying team strengths and weaknesses and suggesting, through training and development, how best to perform specific tasks and functions within a team;

■ Providing a common Team Role language team members can use to discuss team effectiveness; and

■ Identifying and understanding the organisational culture as a result of the team members' role overview.

The training modules required by SARS to support the business process exercise embody a range of elements. These include understanding Team Roles and decision-making; planning and goal-setting; understanding the SARS-specific business case for change; conducting effective team meetings; measuring success; valuing diversity; and developing coaching and empowerment. All these goals and activities are well aligned with the purpose and use of the Belbin Teaming Model.

In conclusion, the Belbin model allows for the integration of training content with actual day-to-day job activities and supports the outcomes-based training methodology and NQF quality and competency assurance standards so important to the South African situation today.

10 Developing team roles in a range of organisations

Brian F. Davis
Worsley Associates Ltd, UK

I have been associated with the Belbin theory of creating effective well-balanced teams for many years and what follows is a personal experience of introducing Belbin Team Roles into organisations in both the public and private sectors throughout the UK.

One matter that constantly intrigues me is the number of people I frequently encounter, often in very senior positions within organisations, who really have little or no idea of the richness, variety, and differences that individuals bring to the workplace. In equal measure is their lack of awareness of the advantages for all concerned of identifying and harnessing these differences in order to create effective well-balanced teams. Perhaps even more important are the consequences for individuals, groups and, indeed, the organisation itself of putting together a number of people merely on the basis they can perform, or can be trained to perform, the required tasks.

This has been graphically demonstrated to me on more than one occasion, but particularly so whilst working with a major plc when I was asked to develop 21 members into 3 effective well-balanced 7-person teams. A not too difficult task of course, using Interplace® and some relevant exercises, but I was taken aback when requested by the organisation to ensure that 7 named members of the 21 were to be considered an existing 'team' and not to be split up in any circumstances. This effectively meant I could use the distinct advantages of the Interplace® system to develop 14 individuals into 27-person teams, but not to alter the construction of the 'team' consisting of the 7 named individuals.

I was initially reluctant to take on the commission, pointing out the obvious disadvantages of such a restriction, but was eventually persuaded to do so. Those familiar with Dr Belbin's theory will appreciate the situation I was facing; those of you who may be less familiar may be intrigued by what occurred.

Having produced the Team Role profiles, I immediately recognized it would be almost impossible to develop the seven named people into an effective well-balanced team. They comprised three males, all of whom scored highly as Shapers, and four females of varying contributions. As those familiar with the Belbin theory will appreciate, three high-scoring Shapers in a seven-person team is usually a recipe for disaster, and so it turned out to be.

During a leadership exercise, the three Shapers couldn't agree who was to lead the 'team', each vying for control; they hijacked the flip charts and the marker pens and literally struggled between themselves to write down objectives and priorities. Each wanted his or her own ideas adopted by the 'team'. They ignored the suggestions, ideas, protestations, and any desire for involvement by the females, one of whom eventually left the room in disgust. They failed to achieve a satisfactory result when compared with the other two seven-person teams. I consider I failed in my attempt to create an effective well-balanced team, but I never believed I really had any chance from the outset.

With the aid of Interplace® any of us could have predicted the likely outcome of this attempt to create a team, without exposing any of its members to the trauma of an exercise. It subsequently transpired that the manager of this seven-person team considered there was a problem and wanted the training and development consultant, me, to identify what was wrong. I could have told him what was wrong, and perhaps more pertinently, he could have discovered for himself had he seen the Belbin Team Role profiles.

This experience is not confined to having too many Shapers in a team, it also applies to groups where there is an imbalance of Team Role contributions or where there is an omission, and as outlined earlier, graphically demonstrates the folly of choosing teams merely on the basis that the members can perform the necessary tasks.

11 The story of a personal transformation

Barrie Watson (Managing Director) *

CERT Consultancy & Training, UK

When invited to contribute a case study describing the practical application of the Belbin Team Role model I eagerly accepted, but was then faced with the dilemma of deciding which one to use of the many available to me.

In the end I decided that the most appropriate case was to describe how Team Roles made an impact on me as a person, a manager, and a human resource management consultant. Recalling the period before I was introduced to Meredith Belbin and the Team Role model, I was quite confident about my prowess as a leader. I felt I knew myself pretty well and knew how to get the best out of others – after all, I had swotted up on Maslow, Hertzberg, McGregor, and others.

The revelations from the theory of Team Roles and results from the Self-Perception Inventory (SPI) produced a rude awakening, for I came to the conclusion I wasn't the consultative, calm, analytical, logical, and caring person I thought I was. My profile was that of the hard-driving, outspoken, persuasive, intuitive entrepreneur, with little feeling for the real needs and motivations of others (Shaper/Resource Investigator). This fact was strongly reinforced when the Observer Assessment facility was introduced as part of the Interplace® system.

Some serious navel gazing and reflection on my past experiences helped to shed a lot of light on why things had worked out as they had. I became clearer about why I had been successful in some aspects of building my businesses and managing people and, sometimes, spectacularly unsuccessful.

Not being one to dwell too much on the past, I quickly turned to the future and decided what I would do differently. Armed with this new knowledge, it soon

* Previously chairman of The Floreat Marketing Group and finance director of NARF Ltd.

became clear that changes would have to be made. This meant breaking a few well-established habits like *striving* to be the best at everything, or maybe more truthfully *pretending* to be the best. I tried new approaches, such as saying to my Monitor Evaluator colleague 'You had better give this your close scrutiny and let me know if you see any flaws in it before I go ahead', or to my Plant co-director, 'I'm stuck with this, can you see a different angle?'

Such actions didn't come naturally, as my style is more akin to saying 'Let's get the plane off the ground. We can finish designing the wings once we are up there.' (This is actually how New Zealand psychologist Dawie Gouws actually described me to his colleagues. What a perceptive man he is!)

This new approach very quickly yielded results. I found it a great relief to be able to admit my weaknesses and try not to conceal them. My colleagues seemed to find a new sense of purpose and fulfilment and felt more valued. Playing to my natural strengths also reaped other rewards, and not just emotionally, the business prospered. This was not the end of the story, however. It was just the beginning, as I passionately set about helping other individuals, teams, and organisations to reap the same benefits.

Do unto others

Fifteen years on, I can say that I have had a great deal of success in applying the Belbin methodology in over 20 countries around the world with organisations covering both the public and private sectors and ranging in size from less than 50 to over 200,000 employees.

In all of these cases the outcomes have, more or less, replicated my personal experiences and successes. The results bear testimony to this, with organisations consistently reporting tangible performance improvements, many of which have been publicly recognized. For example, organisations I have helped to adopt the Belbin methodology have achieved the accolade of winning Britain's Best Factory Award[**] 3 out of 4 years. It may be a coincidence, but I don't think so.

In analysing the factors contributing to the performance improvements achieved, one factor has consistently emerged. People at all levels, from senior executive to shop floor, enthusiastically embrace the Team Role model and have found the Belbin methodology as easy to apply as I did.

[**] The Best Factory Awards are sponsored by Management Today in association with Cranfield School of Management.

Glossary

Anxiety   Anxiety is measured on six scales of the 16PF. Anxious individuals are easily aroused. Where anxiety is allied with strong scores on self-control and discipline (measured on two scales of the 16PF), it tends to be converted into energy and drive. Where the discipline is low, anxiety is inclined either to exert an unsettling effect on others or to result in an unacceptably high level of inner stress.

Anxious Extrovert   Someone high in both anxiety and extroversion.

Anxious Introvert   Someone high in both anxiety and introversion.

Back-Up Team Role   A Team Role to which an individual has some natural affinity other than his primary Team Role.

Chairman (Later changed to Co-ordinator)   As a Team Role, specifies controlling the way in which a team moves towards the group objectives by making the best use of team resources; recognizing where the team's strengths and weaknesses lie; and ensuring that the best use is made of each team member's potential.

Company Worker (Later changed to Implementer)   As a Team Role, specifies turning concepts and plans into practical working procedures; and carrying out agreed plans systematically and efficiently.

Completer–Finisher   As a Team Role, specifies ensuring that the team is protected as far as possible from mistakes of both commission and omission; actively searching for aspects of work which need a more than usual degree of attention; and maintaining a sense of urgency within the team.

Constructs   A set of related ideas and concepts which characterize an individual's outlook on the world. These are elicited by examining the pattern of discriminations an individual makes in sorting through material which is inherently capable of assuming different meanings. The development of construct theory owes much to G.A. Kelly and his *Psychology of Personal Constructs* (New York: Norton, 1955). Kelly's approach relied on a technique known as the Repertory Grid. This method, requiring a continuing intervention between a professionally trained person and a subject, tended to be too slow and costly for most industrial purposes. The PPQ was developed as an alternative method. The constructs of managers to which reference is made in this book refer solely to material generated by the PPQ. *Positive* constructs refer to reasons for liking something; *negative* constructs refer to reasons for dislike.

CTA (Critical Thinking Appraisal)   A test designed jointly by Goodwin Watson, Professor Emeritus of Social Psychology and Education of Columbia University, and Edward M. Glaser of Edward Glaser and Associates, Consulting Psychologists, Los Angeles. The CTA comprises five sections which measure Inference, the ability to discriminate between degrees of truth or falsity from given data; Recognition of Assumptions, the ability to recognize unstated assumptions or presuppositions in given statements; Deduction, the ability to reason accurately from given statements or premises; Interpretation, the ability to weigh evidence and to distinguish between warranted and unwarranted generalizations; and Evaluation of Arguments, the ability to distinguish between arguments which are strong and relevant and those which are weak or irrelevant to a particular question at issue.

The CTA contains one hundred items which have to be completed in fifty minutes, although in practice the time limit was not rigidly enforced. About ninety-five percent of respondents completed all items of the test. The offer was sometimes made of £10 to anyone who obtained full marks (or who got all items wrong!). This remained unclaimed as no one succeeded in achieving a perfect set of answers.

EME (Executive Management Exercise)   The EME was developed by Ben Aston at Henley as a management game. The aim was 'to create a high-intensity reference experience that integrated many management skills that are otherwise treated on a fragmentary basis.' The EME was an interacting game comprising between six and eight *companies*, each of which had six members. Performance depended not only on the decisions made within the *company* but also on the decisions made by other *companies*, in respect of both the home and export markets. Financial returns, made available through a computer, gave results over a period of twelve 'quarters' and the aim was to finish with the largest possible share of available assets. 'Market Research' could be bought and decisions could be made on recruiting salesmen, advertising, investing in research, holding stocks and setting prices. The EME also made provision for transactions with 'banks' and, in more recent years, for negotiations with 'unions' and with 'government'. Over a decade the EME has undergone a period of continuous development but, whatever the differences, results have been generally a fair reflection of *company* or team effectiveness.

Extroversion   Refers to a characteristic type of personality, first identified by Jung, whose interests are directed outwards towards the external world around them rather than towards inner thoughts and feelings. Measured by five of the sixteen scales of the 16PF.

Extrovert   Someone high in extroversion. Extroverts are now known to have distinctive psychophysiological characteristics tending to have high sensory threshold levels. They require more intense stimulation for any given response and their responses tend to fade relatively quickly. Extroverts tend to become bored easily or they adjust to this susceptibility by keeping up a continuous search for active stimulation.

Functional Role   The role that a member of a team performs in terms of the specifically technical demands placed upon him. Typically, team members are chosen for functional roles on the basis of their experience and without regard to any personal characteristics or aptitudes that fit them for additional tasks within the team.

Implementer   The later name given to Company Worker.

Introversion   Discovered by Jung as applying to a type of personality dominated by inner thoughts and feelings rather than by interest in the outer world of men and things. Measured by five of the sixteen scales of the 16PF.

Introvert   Someone high in introversion. Introverts tend to have low stimulus thresholds; they respond strongly to small inputs of stimulus and dislike strong stimulus intensities. They do not get bored easily. Introverts tend to produce deep thinkers and highly creative individuals. They tend to be vulnerable to strong pressures.

Monitor Evaluator   As a Team Role, specifies analysing problems; and evaluating ideas and suggestions so that the team is better placed to take balanced decisions.

16PF   Otherwise known as the Cattell Personality Inventory. This test is a self-reporting questionnaire containing 187 statements in terms of which the respondent must choose between three possible answers. The 16PF is so named because it comprises sixteen personality factors, albeit one of which covers intelligence. The remaining fifteen deal with dimensions of personality that are best known for the words that describe extreme scores at both ends of the dimensions, although these words can be misleading if scale is considered in isolation. The scales are reserved/outgoing, emotional/calm, humble/assertive, serious/happy-go-lucky, expedient/conscientious, shy/bold, tender-minded/tough-minded, trusting/suspicious, meticulous/imaginative, natural/shrewd, confident/apprehensive, conservative/radical, dependent/self-sufficient, uncontrolled/controlled and relaxed/tense.

The 16PF generates a number of so-called second-order factors which combine scores from several scales. The second-order factors referred to in this book are creative disposition, extroversion–introversion and anxiety–stability.

Plant   As a Team Role, specifies advancing new ideas and strategies with special attention to major issues; and looking for possible breaks in approach to the problems with which the group is confronted.

PPQ   The initials of this test stand for Personal Preference Questionnaire. The test was developed by the Industrial Training Research Unit at Cambridge as a means of giving leads on personality and outlook that would be complementary to the information derived from a self-reporting questionnaire (i.e. the 16PF). The PPQ is an open-ended test; in other words the respondent has to create his own responses rather than choose between given alternatives. The test comprises fifty pairs of well-known names (e.g. Mohammed Ali/Henry Cooper, Stan Laurel/ Oliver Hardy), and the respondent is asked to indicate which of the pair is preferred and to give a reason (whether positive or negative) for making the choice. These reasons could be classified with the aid of a PPQ dictionary into five principal categories, each of which contains four sub-groups. The categories are Talent (sub-groups: Ability, Brain, Originality, Versatility); Achievement (sub-groups: Attainment, Competitiveness, Determination, Consistency); Personality (sub-groups: Nice Guy, Flamboyance, Social Capacity, Humour); Justice (sub-group: Fair Play, Integrity, Respectability, Ethics); and Subjective Factors (sub-groups: Clan, Physical Reasons, Empathy, Reaction). Scores in the sub-groups are referred to as constructs. Interpretation of the test scores is facilitated by data available on response norms in the sub-groups for any total response level.

The PPQ is available in forms that suit various countries and different culture levels. So far there are three UK, one international (intellectual), one Australian and one Nigerian editions.

Primary Team Role That Team Role to which an individual has the greatest affinity.

Psychometric Tests These refer to human facilities that lend themselves to measurement. Mental ability, personality, character; and orientation can all be examined by standard tests which yield measured bits of information. Although these tests cannot cover every aspect of the person, their advantage lies in the standardized nature of the information they yield. Individuals can be compared with one another on similar measures; the information has good storage life, is easily retrieved, and lends itself to long-term research and validation.

Resource Investigator As a Team Role, specifies exploring and reporting on ideas, developments and resources outside the group; creating external contacts that may be useful to the team and conducting any subsequent negotiations.

Shaper As a Team Role, specifies shaping the way in which team effort is applied; directing attention generally to the setting of objectives and priorities; and seeking to impose some shape or pattern on group discussion and on the outcome of group activities.

Specialist Someone who supplies knowledge and skills in rare supply and who prefers to contribute on that limited front. As a Team Role it was discovered only after the Henley experiments ended and practical work began.

Stability Measured in six scales of the 16PF and in effect the opposite of anxiety. Stable individuals tend to be easy-going and acceptable to a wide range of people. They can also be casual and lazy and are unlikely to give of their best except under pressure.

Stable Extrovert Someone high in both stability and extroversion.

Stable Introvert Someone high in both stability and introversion.

Syndicate   A group of managers brought together to promote their mutual learning. Each syndicate at Henley contained ten or eleven members and lasted for the duration of the course.

Teamopoly   Teamopoly was developed as an experience offered to those attending management team seminars to enable them to put their newly acquired knowledge and insights into practice. Each *company* comprised four members, with either four or five *companies* taking part in the exercise which usually lasted five hours. Teamopoly was founded on the principles of the well-known game Monopoly but there were some essential differences. All property could change hands only as a result of auction, tender or negotiation. The moves were determined in advance and each *Company* was informed of its moves, so that it could assess their implications before each session of board play. A number of other changes to the rules minimized the element of luck in the game. The scheduling of activities created a great deal of pressure on the *companies* and this sense of pressure was made greater by composing *companies* in such a way that in human terms their membership was unbalanced and therefore likely to create difficulties. Since the game was of more limited character than the EME some members learned to live with these difficulties and to make personal adjustments (team-role sacrifices) in the interests of *company* performance.

Team Role   This describes a pattern of behaviour characteristic of the way in which one team member interacts with another where his performance serves to facilitate the progress of the team as a whole. Only eight useful types of contribution were discovered. These were Chairman, Shaper, Plant, Company Worker, Team Worker, Monitor Evaluator, Resource Investigator and Completer. Each of these Team Roles was associated with characteristic types of personality as measured by the tests used in the experiments.

Team Worker   As a Team Role, specifies supporting members in their strengths (e.g. building on suggestions); underpinning members in their shortcomings; improving communications between members and fostering team spirit generally.

Test Battery   A group of psychometric tests devised to measure in conjunction with one another some broad areas of human characteristics. The test battery used in these studies was put together to yield data that might usefully predict managerial performance and effectiveness. The constituents of the battery were the Watson-Glaser Critical Thinking Appraisal (Form YM), the Cattell 16PF (Form A, 1962 edition) – the 16PF 1967–1968 anglicized edition was abandoned as yielding less satisfactory data – and the PPQ.

Books that figured as the background to the Henley study

Adizes, Ichak, 1981. How to Solve the Mismanagement Crisis: Diagnosis and Treatment of Management Problems. 1981. Adizes Institute, San Diego.

Ardrey, R., 1971. The Social Contract. Fontana, London.

Bales, R.F., 1950. Interaction Process Analysis: a Method for the Study of Small Groups. (Cambridge, Massachusetts. Addison Wesley.

Handy, C., 1979. Gods of Management. Pan Books, London.

Hollander, E.P., 1978. Leadership Dynamics. The Free Press, New York.

Janis, I.L., 1972. Victims of Group Think. Houghton Mifflin, Boston.

Jay, A., 1969. Management and Machiavelli. Hodder and Stoughton, London.

Jay, A., 1972. Corporation Man. Jonathan Cape, London.

Kellner, P., Lord Crowther-Hunt, 1980. The Civil Servants: an Inquiry into Britain's Ruling Class. Macdonald, London.

Likert, R., 1967. The Human Organization: Its Management and Value. McGraw-Hill, New York.

Lippitt, G.L., 1969. Organization Renewal. Appleton-Century-Croft, New York.

Margulies, N., Wallace, J., 1973. Organization Choice. Scott Foresman, Glenview, Ill.

Mintzberg, H., 1973. The Nature of Managerial Work. Harper and Row, San Francisco.

Rackham, N., Honey, P., Colbert, M.J., 1971. Developing Interactive Skills. Wellens Publishing, Guilsborough.

Ramsden, P., 1973. Top-Team Planning. Cassell and Associated Business Programmes, London.

Woodcock, M., 1979. Team Development Manual. Gower Press, Farnborough.

Index